COMPANY LAW AND SECRETARIAL PRACTICE

K GOWRI | ASSISTANT PROFESSOR | NEHRU ARTS AND SCIENCE COLLEGE | COTIMBATORE | TAMILNADU

Contents

Preface

In view of increasing emphasis on adherence to norms of good corporate governance, Company Law assumes an added importance in the corporate legislative milieu, as it deals with the structure, management, administration and conduct of affairs of Companies.

This textbook is published to aid the students in preparing the paper on Company Law for Executive Programme. It is part of the educational kit and takes the students step by step through each phase of preparation emphasizing key concepts, principles, pointers and procedures. Company Secretaryship being a professional course, the examination standards are set very high, with a focus on knowledge of concepts, their application, procedures and case laws, for which sole reliance on the contents of this study material may not be enough. This study material may, therefore, be regarded as the basic material and must be read along with the Bare Acts, Rules, Regulations, and Case Law.

Prologue

I am m glad to present this book, especially designed to serve the needs of the students. The book has been written keeping in mind the general weakness in understanding the fundamental concept of the topic. The book is self-explanatory and adopts the "Teach Yourself" style. The language of the book is quite easy and understandable based on a scientific approach. Any further improvement in the contents of the book by making corrections, omissions and inclusion is keen to be achieved based on suggestions from the reader for which the author shall be obliged.

I look forward to receiving valuable suggestions from professors of various educational institutions, other faculty members and students for the improvement of the quality of the book. The reader may feel free to send in their comments and suggestions.

CHAPTER ONE

INTRODUCTION

Company – Definition – Characteristics – Lifting the Corporate Veil – Advantages of Incorporation – Administration through Various Types of Machinery of the Companies Act.

1.1 INTRODUCTION

A company is a legal entity that is separated and distinct from its members and shareholders. A company is enforced by certain rules and regulations of laws for achieving the targeted goal. Without guidelines or laws, it is directionless and becomes a chaotic condition. At first in France, the word "company" was used for the body of soldiers. After 1500 years, the word company became famous in the business. At that time group of businessmen was called a company. A company can buy property, make contracts, employ people or be used. According to the law, anything that is capable of rights and duties is a person and thus has a personality. According to the law, there are two types of the person such as- natural and artificial person. Human beings are known as natural persons and corporations or companies are known as artificial persons. When a company registered itself by the company act, it can able to achieve the status of a person who can buy, lend money, defend suit and file, sell goods and also can hold property. We can explain the meaning of a company like this-when two people want to do business and are not interested to make a partnership because of its liabilities then they can go to the registered office of companies and fill out the company creation form to pay the fees. And then the registrar will register their company with an independent identity. The first Indian Act, regarding companies, was the Joint Stock Companies Act of 1850. This was based upon the English Act of 1844. In this act, the principle of limited liabilities was introduced in India.

Description:

The term company is used to describe an association of several persons, formed for some common purpose and registered according to the law relating to companies. Section 3(1)(i) of the Companies Act, 1994 states that a company means," a company formed and registered under this Act or an existing company."

Lord Justice Lindley defines a company as follows: "By a company is meant an association of many persons who contribute money or money's worth to a common stock so contributed is denoted in money and its capital of the company. The persons who contribute to it or to whom it belongs are members. The proportion of capital to which each member is entitled is in his share."

The Companies Act 2013 of India defines a company as-

A registered association is an artificial legal person, having an independent legal, entity with perpetual succession, a common seal for its signatures, a common capital comprised of transferable shares and carrying limited liability.

1.According to Justice James, "A company is an association of persons united for a common object."

2.According to Lord Lindley, "By a 'company' is meant an association of many persons who contribute money or money's worth to common stock and employ it for some common purpose. The common stock so contributed is denoted in money and is the capital of the company. The persons who contribute to it or to whom it belongs are members. The proportion of capital to which each partner is entitled is his share."

3.According to Kimball and Kimball, "A corporation is by nature an artificial person created or authorized by the legal stature for some specific purpose."

4.According to Prof. Haney, "A company is an artificial person created by law having a separate entity with a perpetual succession and a common seal."

5.According to James Stephenson, "A company is an association of many persons who contribute money or money's worth to a common stock and employs it in some trade or business, and who share the profit and loss (as the case may be) arising therefrom."

6.According to Section 3 (1) (i) of the Indian Companies Act, 1956. "Company means a company formed and registered under this act or an existing company. 'Existing Company' means a company formed and registered under any of the previous Company Laws."

Few points that should be noted in this definition:

Legal Person: A *legal person* could be a human or a non-human entity which is recognized by law as having legal rights and is subject to obligations.

A person or a group of persons: It is no more required to be an association of persons to form a company. A company can also be started as a single-person company (one-person company).

Definition of Company

In the legal sense, a company is an association of both natural and artificial persons (and is incorporated under the existing law of a country). In terms of the Companies Act, 2013 (Act No. 18 of 2013) a "company" means a company incorporated under this Act or any previous company law [Section 2(*20*)].

1.1.1 EVOLUTION OF COMPANY LAW IN INDIA

India has received several enactments from England. Company law is one such enactment which was embraced by England. In 1850 the first Company enactment was presented in India for the registration of a joint company which was based on the English Company Act 1844. The idea of limited liability was presented in the English Company Act of 1856 which was later presented in India in the year 1857. The Companies Act was altered a few times between 1850 and 1852 and the Act in 1852 repealed all other Acts and stayed till 1912. The Indian Companies Act of 1913 was based on the British Companies Act of 1908. This Act experienced a few amendments. After independence it was discovered that the Companies Act must be changed to fit into the Indian situation, subsequently Companies Act 1956 was passed. This Act is currently replaced by the Companies Act 2013 which got the assent from the President on 29 August 2013.

1.2 NATURE/ FEATURES/ CHARACTERISTICS

1. An Artificial Person Created by Law:

A company is a creation of law, and is, sometimes called an artificial person. It does not take birth like a natural person but comes into existence through law. But a company enjoys all the rights of a natural person. It has the right to enter into contracts and own property. It can sue others and can be sued. But it is an artificial person, so it cannot take the oath, cannot be presented in court and cannot be divorced or married.

2. Separate Legal Entity:

A company is an artificial person and has a legal entity quite distinct from its members. Being a separate legal entity, it bears its name and acts under a corporate name; it has a seal of its own; its assets are separate and distinct from those of its members.

Its members are its owners but they can be its creditors simultaneously as it has a separate legal entity. A shareholder cannot be held liable for the acts of the company even if he holds virtually the entire share capital. The shareholders are not agents of the company and so they cannot bind it by their acts.

3. Perpetual Succession:

The life of a company is not related to the life of members. Law creates the company and dissolves it. The death, insolvency or transfer of shares of members does not, in any way, affect the existence of a company.

According to Tennyson-

"For men may come, men may go,

But I go on forever."

In the case of a company, it may be said that members may come and members may go but the company goes on. It is a legal person having come into being by law and only law can bring its end and none else.

4. Common Seal:

On incorporation, a company becomes a legal entity with perpetual succession and a common seal. The common seal of the company is of great importance. It acts as the official signature of the company. As the company has no physical form, it cannot sign its name on a contract. The name of the company must be engraved on the common seal. A document not bearing the common seal of the company is not authentic and has no legal importance.

5. Limited Liability:

Limited liability is another important feature of the company. If anything goes wrong with the company his risk is only to the extent of the number of his shares and nothing more. If some amount is uncalled upon a share, he is liable to pay it and not beyond that.

The creditors of a company cannot get their claims satisfied beyond the assets of the company. The liability of members of a company 'limited by guarantee is limited to the amount of guarantee.

6. Transferability of Shares:

A shareholder can transfer his shares to any person without the consent of other members. Under Articles of Association, a company can put certain restrictions on the transfer of shares but it cannot altogether stop it. A private company can put more restrictions on the transferability of shares.

7. Limitation of Work:

The field of work of a company is fixed by its charter. The Memorandum of Association. A company cannot do anything beyond the powers defined in it.

Its action is, therefore, limited. To do the work beyond the memorandum of association, there is a need for its alteration.

8. Voluntary Association for Profits:

A company is a voluntary association of persons to earn profits. It is formed for the accomplishment of some public good and whatsoever profit is divided among its shareholders. A company cannot be formed to carry on activity against public policy and has no profit motive.

9. Representative Management:

The shareholders of the company are widely scattered. All the shareholders can't take part in the management. They leave their task to the representatives of the Board of Directors and the company is managed by the Board of Directors.

10. Termination of Existence:

A company is created by law, carries on its affairs according to law and ultimately is affected by the law. Generally, the existence of a company is terminated using winding up.

1.3 CORPORATE VEIL THEORY

The word company is derived from the Latin word *Com* meaning with or together and *pains* meaning bread, and it originally referred to an association of persons who took their meals together. Today business matters have become more complicated and the word "Company" has assumed greater importance. A company is thus a voluntary association of people who come together to for carrying on some business and share profits therein. Members contribute capital and the profits are distributed among various stakeholders. Thus, a company denotes an association of like-minded persons formed to carry on some business or undertaking. It can be for profit or it can be for a charitable purpose. A company is a body and a legal person having status and personality distinct and separate from that of the members constituting it.

A Company is not a 'person' in the layman's language. It is an organization created by a group of individuals who come together for the purpose of business. It is thus the personification of a group or series of individuals making it a legal person. By the provision of law, a corporation is clothed with a distinct personality. A company being an artificial person, does not have a mind of its own and thus cannot act on its own, it can only act through natural persons or the people who are members of it. The business is carried on by a real person, and for the benefit of, some individuals, i.e., some human beings are the real beneficiaries of the corporate advantages.

However, sometimes the corporation may commit certain fraud or misrepresentation and in such a case, the façade of corporate personality might be removed to identify the persons who arethe really guilty personsrlier elucidated Courts usually follow the principle of the *separate entity* as laid down in Solomon's Case, however, it may be in the interest of the members or the general public to identify and punish the persons who misuse the medium corporate personality.

Thus, where fraudulent and dishonest use is made of the legal entity, the individuals concerned will not be allowed to take shelter behind the corporate personality. The Court will break through the corporate cloak and will look behind the corporate body as if there is no separate existence of the company from its members. Further, if found guilty of any misconduct, it can penalize the members for actions of the company including any pending debt. This is known as **lifting the corporate veil**.

1.3.1 MEANING OF THE CORPORATE VEIL

A legal principle of the corporate veil distinguishes the conduct of corporations and companies from the actions of shareholders. It safeguards the stockholders from liability for the company's conduct. It is not an absolute right; the court might decide whether the shareholder is responsible or not based on the facts and circumstances of the case.

"Shareholders may shelter behind the principle of the corporate veil, certain that their obligation does not extend beyond the value of their shares," according to the Cambridge Dictionary.

1.3.2 COMPANY: A SEPARATE LEGAL ENTITY

Corporate personality is the legal fact that a company is recognized as a legal entity apart from its individuals. A corporation with such recognition and personality would be treated as a distinct legal entity with its own legal identity apart from the members of the firm. A corporation has its name and its own set of rights, duties, obligations, and liabilities. As a result, the corporation and its members are distinguishable, which is usually referred to as a Corporate Veil.

The essential element on which company law is based is the independent legal entity. The legal entity of the firm determines how a company comes into being, as well as how it is handled and operated. The notion of a separate legal body is not new, and there are several instances and litigation on the subject and its jurisdiction. There are two landmark decisions on separate legal entities, one of which is Salomon vs. Salomon and the other is Lee vs. Lee, both of which are foreign yet relevant and acknowledged globally.

Case – Salomon vs. Salomon & Co. Ltd. (1897) A.C. 22

Facts – Salomon was a solo owner running a boot and leather merchant business when he decided to establish his company, Salomon Ltd., with members consisting of his own family and himself. The company had collapsed and was losing money. The firm fell into liquidation after its business collapsed. Salomon's right of recovery, backed by a floating charge on debentures, had priority over the business's creditors, who claimed that Salomon and his company "Salomon Company" were the same person. On behalf of unsecured creditors, the liquidator claimed that the business was a fabrication and that it was simply a Salomon agent.

As the principal of the Co., Salomon was held responsible for the company's debt and unsecured creditors. As a result, the question was if he would personally responsible for the business's debt, regardless of whether the firm was a separate legal entity.

Held – It was held that the firm was determined to be a legitimate and legal entity that complied with all legal criteria. It had a distinct identity from its members, and as a result, unsecured creditors were to be paid ahead of secured debentures.

Case – Lee vs. Air Farming Ltd. (1960) AC 12

Facts – Lee, is a licensed pilot who established Lee's Air Farming Ltd. to continue the business of aerial top-dressing. The share capital of the company was made up of 3000 shares, each worth one Euro. Lee held 2999 of the 3000 shares in the company.

Lee was also the company's director. He had unlimited authority over the company's operations. He was the one who made all of the company's contract judgments. For the insurance of its employees, the firm engaged in many arrangements with other companies, insurance agencies, and so on. For the personal insurance held and taken by Lee, the premiums were paid from the bank account of the company, and that sum was deducted from Lee's account in the company's book.

Lee was a pilot in addition to being the company's director and he died while flying the plane during an aerial top-dressing mission. His widowed wife sought reimbursement under the New Zealand Workers' Compensation Act, 1992, for her husband's death while on the job. The firm argued that because Lee was the company's owner and held the most shares, his wife was not entitled to any compensation.

Held – The court decided that Lee was a different person from the firm he established, and therefore his widow should be properly compensated. This decision is significant in terms of the Indian Companies Act, 2013 because it establishes the precedent that a company is a distinct legal entity capable of contracting with its members.

1.3.4 THE PRINCIPLE OF LIFTING OF CORPORATE VEIL

A company is seen as a distinct legal entity apart from its members, however, in reality, it is an association of people who are the beneficial company owners and its corporate property. This illusion is established through a veil, which is referred to as the Corporate Veil. Piercing /lifting of corporate veil entails disregarding the notion that a corporation is a separate legal entity with its own identity (Corporate personality). This idea disregards the business's distinct identity & focuses on the actual owners or real people in control of the organization.

A company's distinct personality is a statutory privilege which should be used for a lawful purpose exclusively. Persons shall not be able to escape behind the curtain of corporate personality anytime a fraudulent or dishonest use of the legal organization is done. The competent authorities will pierce the company's shell and sue the persons who have done or committed such a crime or offence. The breaking of the curtain is referred to as a Lifting of the Corporate Veil.

1.3.5 STATUTORY PROVISIONS RELATING TO LIFTING OF CORPORATE VEIL

Numerous sections of the Companies Act, 2013 have been amended that aim to identify the individual who is accountable for any such improper/illegal action. Those individuals are most commonly referred to as "officers in default" u/s 2(60) of the Companies Act which covers those in positions like directors or senior management roles. Below mentioned are a few examples of such frameworks:

1. Misstatement in Prospectus of the Company – Companies offer securities for sale by publishing prospectuses. The prospectus produced u/s 26 provides essential notes about the firm, like facts about shares and debentures, the names of directors, the company's principal goals and current activity. If someone attempts to provide misleading or untrue/ inaccurate representations in a prospectus of the Co., he is liable to the penalty, imprisonment, or both stipulated u/s 26 (9), 34, and 35 of the Act, depending on the circumstances.

2.Reduction of No. of Members below the Statutory Minimum – If the minimum number no. of members of a company falls below 2 (for private companies), or below 7 (for public companies), the company can continue to operate for 6 months while the number is so reduced, and every person who is a member of the company during that time, knowing that the minimum number of members has been reduced. If the grace period of 6 months has expired, the corporation and its members will be held accountable and can claim for the sum they earned during those 6 months, or the firm may be sued severally.

3.Failure to Refund Application Fees – According to Section 39 (3) of the Act, if the directors of the company fail to repay the application money (without interest) within 120 days when the Co. fails to allot shares, they will be jointly and severally accountable to pay back the money along with interest of 6% p.a. from the date of expiry of 130 days.

4.Misperception of the Name of the Company – According to section 12, an officer of a corporation who signs any bill of trade, hundi, promissory note, or check where the name of the organization is not referenced in the recommended way could be held personally accountable to the holder of the bill of trade, hundi, etc. unless it is appropriately paid by the company.

5.Fraudulent Trading – Section 339 of the Companies Act, 2013 If, during a company's winding-up, it seems that any business of the company was conducted to defraud the company's creditors or any other persons, or for any illegal purpose, the Tribunal, on the application of the Official Liquidator, the Company Liquidator, or any creditor or contributory of the company believes it is appropriate, may proclaim that any individual who is or has been a company's director, manager, or officer, or any individuals who were intentionally parties to the carrying on of the business in the manner aforesaid will be responsible personally, with no limitation of liability, for all or all of the company's debts or other liabilities, as directed by the Tribunal. Every individual knowing that fraud shall be punished with imprisonment for a period of up to 2 years or a fine of up to Rs. 50,000/-, or both.

6.For Investing Ownership of the Company – According to Section 216 of the Act, the Central Government may appoint Inspectors to examine and report on the company's membership to determine the real persons who are financially engaged in the firm and who influence its policies. As a result, the Central Government might ignore the corporate veil.

7.Inducing Persons to Invest Funds in the Company – According to Section 36 of the Act, anyone who makes false, fraudulent, misleading, or inaccurate representations or promises to another person or hides relevant material from another person to induce him in doing any of the following: -

- An agreement to acquire, disposes of, subscribe to, or underwrite securities.
- An agreement to guarantee gains to any of the parties based on the return of securities or changes in the value of securities.
- An agreement to receive credit from any bank or financial organization.

In certain cases, the corporate personality might be neglected to identify the actual guilty party and hold him solely accountable.

8.To Furnish False tatements – Under Section 448 of the Act, if any person makes false or untrue representations in any necessary return, report, certificate, financial statement, prospectus, statement, or another document, or hides any relevant or material truth, he is responsible u/s 447 of the Act. The corporate veil must be lifted to find the true guilty individual who authorized such documents to be disclosed in the name of the firm.

9.Repeated Defaults – According to Section 449 of the Act, if a company or an officer of a company commits an offence shall be punished by fine or imprisonment and commits the same offence within three years, the company and officer must pay twice the penalty in addition to any custodial sentence imposed for such offence.

10. In the Case of Ultra-Virus Acts – Every company is required to operate by its AoA, MoA, and the **Companies Act, 2013**. Any activity performed outside the jurisdiction of either is considered to be "ultra-virus" inappropriate or beyond the certified scope. Penalties may be imposed if the company's operations are found to be illegal. Directors and other officers of a corporation will be personally liable for all acts performed on its behalf if they are ultra-virus of the corporation.

11.In the case where Companies Internationally Avoiding Legal Obligations – Wherever it is discovered that an incorporated company is attempting to escape legal responsibilities, or that the incorporation of a company is being exploited to avoid the force of law, the courts have the right to reject the business's legal identity and continue as if it never existed. Liabilities might be imposed on the people involved.

1.3.6 JUDICIAL GROUNDS FOR LIFTING OF CORPORATE VEIL

Case Studies

Gilford Motor Company vs. Horne (1933) T CH 935

Facts – Mr Horne served as the former Managing Director of Gilford Motor Home Company Ltd. His employment contract included a clause prohibiting him from soliciting the company's clients after he left. Mr Horne was dismissed from his employment and post. Following that, he formed a competitive firm with his wife, himself, and one of his friends as the only owners. Horne's business is less expensive than Gilford's. The stockholders began approaching Gilford Motor Company's consumers. Gilford had no legal rights against Horne's firm, only against Horne himself. Gilford sued or started legal action against Horne, alleging that his firm was an attempt to avoid legal duties by recruiting consumers.

Held – The Corporation was put up to avoid Horne's contractual accountabilities and was utilized as a fraud tool to hide Mr Horne's illegal acts, according to the court. The court also ordered an injunction against him, piercing the corporate veil.

- **Invocation of the Principal of the Agency**

The principle of the corporate veil may be disregarded when it is necessary to identify the principle and agent in connection with an inappropriate activity undertaken by the agency.

RG Films Ltd. (1953)

Facts – An American business sponsored the production of a movie in India under the name of a British company, and the president of an American company owned 90% of the shares in the British firm. The corporation had no additional assets beyond its registered office and no employees. Following that, the Board of Trade declined to register the movie as a British Film since the British business was only acting as an agent for an American corporation.

Held – The ruling was upheld because the British firm was only acting as a nominee for the American corporation. Here, the court ordered the lifting of the corporate veil and it was determined that the theory of distinct legal entity does not imply that the business would operate as a simple agent of the shareholders.

- **Against Public Policy**

When a company's actions violate public policy or the public interest, courts have the authority to pierce the veil and hold those who are personally accountable. The right basis for piercing the corporate personality is to safeguard public policy.

Connors Bros vs. Connors (1940)

Facts – In this matter, the actions done by the company's members prompted the court to invoke the principle of the lifting of the corporate veil to penalize the offenders since the firm was created to carry out an activity that was against public policy. The concept was used upon the managing director who abused his position by acting in a way that was against public policy.

Held – Since the people who were de facto residents of Germany, which was at war with the British at the period, the House of Lords ruled that the firm was an enemy company. The alien firm was not permitted to continue with the act. It was regarded as against state policy because it directly or indirectly involved sending money to the enemy.

- **Determining the True (enemy) Character of the Company / Avoid Welfare Legislation**

Where the goal of forming a business is to solely make profits. A corporation will not intentionally try to do good for society. It may, although, choose to inflict harm instead.

Daimler Co. Ltd. vs. Continental Tyre and Rubber Co. Ltd. (1916)

Facts – A German business formed a private company in England for selling motor tyres made in Germany. The German firm owns virtually all of the business's shares, and all of the company's directors are Germans.

Held – The House of Lords held that the firm was an enemy company for trade since its effective control or administration was in the arms of Germans. The court determined that if there is a trade between them, it would be against public policy, and so the firm will not be permitted to proceed with the action.

- **Tax Evasion (Protection of Revenue)**

It is the responsibility of every earner to pay their fair share of taxes. From the perspective of the law, a corporation is no different from a person. Anyone who tries to escape this responsibility illegally is considered to be committing an offence.

CIT vs. Meenakshi Mills Ltd. AIR 1967 SC 819

Held – If a corporation is created only to avoid paying taxes, then the principle of the lifting of the corporate veil may be invoked. The Supreme Court decided in the case of ***Income Tax Commissioner, Madras vs Sri Meenakshi Mills, Madurai*** that the Income Tax authorities had the power to pierce the corporate veil in this instance.

- **Negligent Activities**

Every corporate entity establishes a distinction between holding and subsidiary companies. Under Indian company law, holding companies are the ones that have a say in the constitution of the Board of Directors or own more than half of the entire share capital of a subsidiary company. For instance, Tata Sons are a holding company, with Tata Motors, TCS, and Tata Steel as subsidiaries.

1.4 INCORPORATION OF A COMPANY

The incorporation of a company refers to the legal process that is used to form a corporate entity or a company. An incorporated company is a separate legal entity on its own, recognized by the law. These corporations can be identified with terms like 'Inc' or 'Limited' in their names. It becomes a corporate legal entity completely separate from its owners.

1.4.1 STEPS IN INCORPORATION OF A COMPANY

A group of seven or more people can come together to form a public company whereas, only two are needed to form a private company. The following steps are involved in the incorporation of a company.

1. Ascertaining Availability of Name:

The first step in the incorporation of any company is to choose an appropriate name. A company is identified through the name it registers. The name of the company is stated in the memorandum of association of the company. The company's name must end with 'Limited' if it's a public company and 'Private Limited' if it's a private company.

To check whether the chosen name is available for adoption, the promoters have to write an application to the Registrar of Companies of the State. A 500 rupee is paid with the application. The Registrar then allows the company to adopt the name given they fulfil all legal documentation formalities within three months.

2. Preparation of Memorandum of Association and Articles of Association:

The memorandum of association of a company can be referred to as its constitution or rulebook. The memorandum states the field in which the company will do business, the objectives of the company, as well as the type of business the company plans to undertake. It is further divided into five clauses.

1. **Name Clause**
2. **Registered Office Clause**
3. **Objects Clause**
4. **Liability Clause**
5. **Capital Clause**

An article of Association is a document that states rules which the internal management of the company will follow. The article creates a contract between the company and its members. The article mentions the rights, duties, and liabilities of the members. It is equally binding on all the members of the company.

3. Printing, Signing and Stamping, Vetting of Memorandum and Articles:

The Registrar of Companies often helps promoters to draw up and draft the memorandum and articles of association. Above all, with promoters who have no previous experience in drafting the memorandum and articles?

Once these have been vetted by the Registrar of Companies, then the memorandum of association and articles of association can be printed. The memorandum and articles are consequently divided into paragraphs and arranged chronologically.

4. Power of Attorney:

To fulfil the legal and complex documentation formalities of incorporation of a company, the promoter may then employ an attorney who will have the authority to act on behalf of the company and its promoters. The attorney will have the authority to make changes to the memorandum and articles and other documents that have been filed with the registrar.

5. Other Documents to be Filed with the Registrar of Companies:

The First – e-Form No.32 – Consent of directors

The Second – e-Form No.18 – Notice of Registered Address

The Third – e-Form No.32. – Particulars of Directors

6. Statutory Declaration in e-Form No.1:

This declaration, furthermore states that 'All the requirements of the Companies Act and the rules thereunder have been compiled with respect of and matters precedent and incidental thereto.'

7. Payment of Registration Fees:

A prescribed fee is to be paid to the Registrar of Companies during incorporation. It depends on the nominal capital of the companies which also have share capital.

8. Certificate of Incorporation:

If the Registrar is completely satisfied that all requirements have been fulfilled by the company that is being incorporated, then he will register the company and issue a certificate of incorporation. As a result, the incorporation certificate provided by the Registrar is definite proof that all requirements of the Act have been met.

1.4.2 WHY INCORPORATION OF A BUSINESS IS NECESSARY?

Incorporation is a government registration process. As a legal entity, the created corporation is given the same powers in law as a 'natural'

So, just like a 'natural person, a corporation can sue and be sued, it can sign contracts and buy and sell property on its own It can be taxed and even commit crimes. This is Why incorporation of a Business is necessary.

1.4.3 WHY INCORPORATING A COMPANY IS NECESSARY?

- Shield yourself from liability.
- Establish Perpetual Existence and Transfer of Ownership.
- Gain Tax Advantage
- Enhance the Company's image
- Improve ability to manage.

1.4.4 ADVANTAGES OF INCORPORATION OF A COMPANY

1. Corporate Personality:

An incorporated company is a legally recognized entity that exists separately from its owners and shareholders, which is different from partnership companies.

Section 34(2) of the Companies Act, 1956 states that from the date of the incorporation of the company, the subscribers to the memorandum and other members shall be a body corporate by the name contained in the memorandum, capable of exercising all the functions of an incorporated company and having perpetual succession and a common seat.

2. Limited Liability:

The Companies Act provides that in event of a company being shut down, the members of the company are solely liable to contribute to the assets and liabilities of the company. It is by the Companies Act – Section 34(2).

However, in the case of companies that have been incorporated, none of its members is legally bound to contribute to anything more than the nominal value of shares held by the member which remain unpaid.

The advantage of having limited liability for its members is one of the major reasons for setting up an incorporated company.

3. Perpetual Succession:

As provided by the Companies Act Section 34(2), an incorporated company has the characteristic of perpetual succession.

Despite any changes in members of the company, the company will be the same entity with the same privileges, immunities, estate, and possessions.

The death or insolvency of individual members does not affect the incorporated company in any way or form. The company will continue to exist indefinitely till the company is shut down.

As the Companies Act states, 'Members may come and members may go, but the company can go on forever.'

4. Transferable Shares:

Section 82 of the companies act states that 'The shares or other interest of any member in a company shall be movable property, transferable in the manner provided by the articles of the company.'

This leads to the investment of funds in shares. It is done so that members can encash shares at any given time upon their will.

It also serves the purpose of providing liquidity to investors. They can sell shares, anytime they are willing to, on the open market or the stock exchange.

5. Separate Property:

An incorporated company as a recognized legal entity is permitted to own its funds and also other assets. 'The property of the company is not the property of shareholders; it is the property of the company.'

'The company is the real person in which the property is vested, and by which it is controlled, managed and disposed of.' And thus, under the law, if a majority shareholder of uses the company's resources for personal reasons, he is liable to be held for criminal misappropriation of company funds.

6. Capacity to Sue:

As a separate legal entity, an incorporated company has the right to sue other people in addition to companies. In turn, it can be sued by other companies and people.

However, the managing directors and other directors are not liable to be sued in the name of the company.

7. Flexibility and Autonomy:

The company has autonomy and independence to form its policies and further, implement them. However, they are subject to the general principles of law, equity and a good conscience.

By the provisions that are mentioned in the Companies Act, Memorandum and Articles of Association.

1.4.5 DISADVANTAGES OF INCORPORATION

There are many disadvantages of Incorporation that business owners should know about: Formalities and Expenses, Corporate Disclosure, Separation of control from ownership, Greater Social, Responsibility, Greater Tax Burden in Certain Cases, and Detailed Winding Up Procedure. Let us discuss them in detail.

1. Formalities and Expenses:

Incorporation of a company is a very complex legal process and it involves a considerable amount of time and money. These elaborate procedures have been established to discourage people from doing business who are not serious and passionate about it.

Even after the incorporation of the company, it has to be run and managed very strictly. By the legal provisions provided by the Companies Act. The returns and other documents have to be registered at the Registrar of Companies.

Certain particular events or activities such as accounts, corporate audits, meetings, borrowing, lending, investment and issue of capital, dividends etc., are necessarily required to be conducted and carried out by the provisions of the Companies Act.

2. Corporate Disclosures:

Despite the extensive legal framework designed to ensure maximum transparency and disclosure of corporate information, the employees and low-level members of the company have restricted access to the company information and higher management.

3. Separation of Control from Ownership:

Members of small shareholders of a company do not have any effective form of control over the functions and decisions of the company.

This happens because the number of people in the company is so large that an individual or even a small group of people cannot have a big effect on the working of the organization.

Thus, the position termed as 'ownership' of the company is just a term that has no real significance. They do not have any active or complete control over the company's workings.

4. Greater Social Responsibility:

Many incorporated companies have a net worth of billions of dollars and thus employ hundreds of thousands of employees. They have a very huge impact on society and these companies often take part in social activities that are part of their CSR (corporate social responsibility) campaigns.

Because of the colossal impact these huge incorporated companies have, they have to follow certain social norms and contribute to the development of society.

5. Greater Tax Burden in Certain Cases:

As compared to other types of companies, incorporated companies have to pay a higher tax. An incorporated company does not get any discounts and any minimum taxable limits.

An incorporated company also has to pay income tax on the whole of its income at a fixed rate whereas other companies are charged at a gradual or slab rate.

1.4.6 THE COMPANIES ACT 2013

1. The Company Act 2013

(*1*) This Act may be called the Companies Act, 2013.

(*2*) It extends to the whole of India.

(*3*) This section shall come into force at once and the remaining provisions of this Act shall come into force on such date as the Central Government may, by notification in the Official Gazette, appoint and different dates may be appointed for different provisions of this Act and any reference in any provision to the commencement of this Act shall be construed as a reference to the coming into force of that provision.

(*4*) The provisions of this Act shall apply to—

(*a*) Companies incorporated under this Act or any previous company law;

(*b*) Insurance companies, except in so far as the said provisions are inconsistent with the provisions of the Insurance Act, 1938 or the Insurance Regulatory and Development Authority Act, 1999;

(*c*) Banking companies, except in so far as the said provisions are inconsistent with the provisions of the Banking Regulation Act, 1949;

(*d*) Companies engaged in the generation or supply of electricity, except in so far as the said provisions are inconsistent with the provisions of the Electricity Act, 2003;

(*e*) any other company governed by any special Act for the time being in force, except in so far as the said provisions are inconsistent with the provisions of such special Act; and

(*f*) Such body corporate, incorporated by any Act for the time being in force, as the Central Government may, by notification, specify on this behalf, subject to such exceptions, modifications or adaptation, as may be specified in the notification.

2. Definitions

In this Act, unless the context otherwise requires, —

(*1*) "abridged prospectus" means a memorandum containing such salient features of a prospectus as may be specified by the Securities and Exchange Board by making regulations on this behalf;

(*2*) "Accounting standards" means the standards of accounting or any addendum thereto for companies or class of companies referred to in section 133;

3) "Alter" or "alteration" includes the making of additions, omissions and substitutions;

(*4*) "Appellate Tribunal" means the National Company Law Appellate Tribunal constituted under section 410;

(*5*) "articles" means the articles of association of a company as originally framed or as altered from time to time or applied in pursuance of any previous company law or this Act;

(*6*) "associate company", about another company, means a company in which that other company has a significant influence, but which is not a subsidiary company of the company having such influence and includes a joint venture company.

Explanation. —for this clause, "significant influence" means control of at least twenty per cent. of total share capital, or business decisions under an agreement;

(*7*) "Auditing standards," means the standards of auditing or any addendum thereto for companies or class of companies referred to in sub-section (*10*) of section 143;

(*8*) "Authorized capital" or "nominal capital," means such capital as is authorized by the memorandum of a company to be the maximum amount of share capital of the company;

(*9*) "Banking company" means a banking company as defined in clause (*c*) of section 5 of the Banking Regulation Act, 1949;

(*10*) "Board of Directors" or "Board", about a company, means the collective body of the directors of the company;

(*11*) "Body corporate" or "corporation" includes a company incorporated outside India but does not include.

1.5 REGISTRATION PROCEDURE UNDER COMPANIES ACT 2013

As per section 7 of the Companies Act,2013, the **incorporation of the company** shall be filed with the Registrar within whose jurisdiction the **registered office of the company** is to be situated. The required documents are as follows.

Memorandum of association (herein referred to as MOA) and **Article of Association** (herein referred to as AOA) which is to be signed by all the subscribers to the memorandum in the prescribed form.

A **declaration** is to be made in the prescribed manner by **an advocate, a chartered accountant, cost accountant** or **company secretary** who is a part of the formation of the company and also by a person named in the article as director, manager or secretary of the company that all the requirements of the act and rules for registration of an association are fulfilled.

An affidavit of each of the **subscribers to the memorandum** and person named as first directors in the article declaring that they have not indulged in any criminal activity during promotion, formation or management of the company neither be found guilty of any fraud or misrepresentation or any breach of duty of any company under present company law or any previous 5-year company law.

The affidavit must also state that all the documents given to the **Registrar for registration of the company** are true to his knowledge that contains all the correct information. If any of such information is found wrong, the person shall be liable for action under section 447 of the Act.

Correspondence address of company till its registration must be established.

All the particulars (name, address, surname, nationality, etc.) of each subscriber to the MOA and person mentioned as first directors in the AOA of the company along with identity proof and for directors **Director Identification Number** must be prescribed in case any subscriber is a company then such details should be prescribed.

Particulars relating to the interest of the first directors of the company in other firms or body corporate along with their consent as a director must also be provided.

After collecting all the information and documents, the registrar shall register all the documents and information given to him and issue a certificate in a prescribed form to ratify the **company proposed incorporated under this act.**

The company will also be provided with a distinct identity in the form of a **Corporate Identification Number** that must also be included in the certificate issued by the Registrar after incorporation is completed.

The company shall keep all the copies of the documents and information provided during registration at its registered of till its dissolution.

Section -8 of the companies act, 2013 deals with the formation of charitable companies whose objectives are charitable. Such companies must be registered under this act as limited companies

CHAPTER TWO

KINDS OF COMPANIES

Kinds of Companies - Classification on the Basis of Incorporation – On the Basis of Members - Private and Public Privileges of a Private Company – Private and Public Company Distinguished – On the basis of Liability – LLP'S – on the Basis of Ownership - Government Company Foreign Company – On the Basis of Control - Holding and Subsidiary Company - Producer Companies

A company is a legal entity formed by a group of individuals to engage in and operate a business—commercial or industrial enterprise. A company may be organized in various ways for tax and financial liability purposes depending on the corporate law of its jurisdiction.

2.1 KINDS OF COMPANY

Companies may be classified into various kinds on the following basis:

1. On the basis of incorporation
2. On the basis of liability
3. On the basis of the number of members
4. On the basis of control
5. On the basis of ownership

2.1.1 ON THE BASIS OF INCORPORATION

On the basis of incorporation companies may be classified into the following three categories:

(i) By Royal Charter-Chartered Companies:

A chartered company is created by the charter or special sanction granted by the Head of the State giving certain exclusive privileges, rights and powers to a distinct body of persons for undertaking commercial activities in specified geographical areas. These rights and privileges are to be enjoyed and the powers are to be used within the terms of the charter.

The British East India Company was formed in England in 1600 and the Dutch East India Company chartered in Holland in 1602 to trade with India the East and Bank of England (1690) are examples of such companies. Since the country attained independence these types of companies do not exist in India.

(ii) Statutory Company:

A statutory company is brought into existence under the Act passed by the legislature of the country or state. Powers, responsibilities, liabilities, objects, scope etc. of such a company are clearly defined under the provisions of the Act, which brings it into existence.

Usually, such companies are established to run enterprises of social or national importance. The Reserve Bank of India, the Industrial Finance Corporation of India, and the Life Insurance Corporation of India are some examples of statutory companies in India.

(iii) Registered Companies:

A registered company is a company, which is organized by getting it registered with the Registrar of Companies under the provisions of the Companies Act of the country concerned. Relevant provisions of the Companies Act govern the formation, working and continuity of such a company.

Most of the companies in the field of industry and commerce are registered companies. In India, such companies are registered under the Indian Companies Act, 1956.

2.1.2 ON THE BASIS OF LIABILITY

On the basis of liability, the company may be classified into:

(a) Limited liability Companies:

(i) Companies limited by shares

(ii) Companies limited by guarantee

(b) Unlimited Liability Companies:

(a) Limited Liability Companies:

Where the liability of the members of a company is limited to the extent of the nominal value of shares held by them, such companies are known as Limited liability companies.

(i) Companies Limited by Shares:

Where the liability of the members of a company is limited by the Memorandum of Association to the amount unpaid on the shares, such a company is called a company limited by shares. In case of winding up of the company, the members cannot be asked to pay more than the amount unpaid on the shares held by them. A company limited by shares may be a public company or a private company.

For example, a shareholder who has paid 75 on a share of the face value of 100 can be called upon to pay the balance of 25 only. Companies limited by shares are by far the most common and may be either public or private.

(ii) Companies Limited by Guarantee:

Where the liability of the members of a company is limited by the Memorandum of Association to such an amount as the members undertake to contribute to the assets of the company in the event of its winding up.

Such types of companies are not formed for profit but are formed for the promotion of art, science, sports, commerce and for cultural activities. Such companies may or may not have share capital. If it has a share capital, it may be a public company or a private company.

(b) Unlimited Liability Companies:

Where the liability of members is not limited, such companies are known as unlimited liability companies. Every member of such a company is liable for its debts in proportion to his interest in the company. Such a company can be converted into a limited liability company after passing a special resolution for conversion and applying to the Registrar of Companies for enrolling it as a limited company.

2.1.3 ON THE BASIS OF THE NUMBER OF MEMBERS:

On the basis of several members, a company may be:

1. Private Company and
2. Public Company.

1. Private Company:

According to Sec. 3(1)(iii) of the Indian Companies Act, 1956, a private company is that company by its articles of association:

(i) limits the number of its members to fifty, excluding employees who are members or ex-employees who were and continue to be members;

(ii) restricts the right of transfer of shares, if any;

(iii) Prohibits any invitation to the public to subscribe for any shares to debenture of the company.

Where two or more persons hold shares jointly, they are treated as a single member.

According to Sec. 12 of the Companies Act, the minimum number of members to form a private company is two. A private company must use the word 'Pvt' after its name.

Features of a Private Company

(i) A private company restricts the right of transfer of its shares. The shares of a private company are not as freely transferable as those of public companies. The articles generally state that whenever a shareholder of a Private company wants to transfer his shares, he must first offer them to the existing members of the company. The price of the shares is determined by the directors. It is done to preserve the family nature of the company's shareholders.

(ii) It limits the number of its members to fifty excluding members who are employees or ex-employees who were and continue to be members. Where two or more persons hold shares jointly they are treated as a single member. The minimum number of members to form a private company is two.

(iii) A private company cannot invite the public to subscribe to its shares or debentures. It has to make a private arrangement to raise its capital or loans.

Advantages of Private Company

A private company enjoys the following advantages over a limited company.

1. A private company is easy to form than a public company. Only two members are sufficient to form a private company.
2. It can start its business immediately after incorporation. A certificate to commence business is not required to be obtained, which is compulsory for a public company.
3. It may pay remuneration to directors and managerial personnel or appoint anyone to the office of profits without any restrictions.
4. As no outsiders are its shareholders it is not required to hold a statutory meeting or file a statutory report.
5. It may give loans to directors without obtaining consent or approval of the Central Government.
6. There is greater flexibility regarding the management and conduct of the business than in a public company.
7. The control and management are generally in the hands of capital owners, which is not the case with a public company.

Special Privilege of Private Company

1. **Number of Members:** A private company can be formed with just two members.
2. **Allotment before Minimum Subscription:** The private company can make an allotment of shares even before the minimum subscription is received.
3. **Prospectus:** Private companies need not issue a prospectus or file statements instead of the prospectus with the Registrar of Companies.
4. **Commencement of Business:** It can commence its business after receiving an incorporation certificate. Whereas a public company can commence business only after receiving the Certificate of Commencement of Business.
5. **Number of Directors:** It requires only two directors.
6. **Statutory Meetings:** Private company is not required to hold statutory meetings and file a statutory report with the Registrar of Companies.
7. **Index of Members:** It is not required to keep and maintain an index of members.
8. **Loan to Directors:** It can grant loans to directors without the permission of the government.
9. **Qualification Shares:** Directors of the private company need not have qualification shares.
10. **No Restriction on the Number of Directors:** The private company can increase its number of directors without the permission of the government.
11. **Appointment of Managing Director:** The private company can appoint a person as managing director, who has already been working as the managing director of another company.
12. **Quorum of Directors Meeting:** Only two directors are sufficient to constitute a quorum.
13. **Retirement of Directors by Rotation:** The directors of a private company need not retire by rotation.
14. **Remuneration of Managers and Directors:** There is no limit on the remuneration of managers and directors of a private company. The change or increase in remuneration can be made without the approval of the Central

Government.

2. Public Company:

According to Section 3(1)(iv) of the Indian Companies Act, 1956 A public company means a company which is not a private company.

If we explain the definition of the Indian Companies Act, 1956 regarding the public company, we note the following:

(i) The articles do not restrict the transfer of shares of the company.

(ii) It does not restrict the maximum number of members in the company.

(iii) It invites the general public to purchase the shares and debentures of the company.

Conversion of a Public Company into a Private Company

As per section 14 of the Companies Act, 2013 a public company may convert itself into a private company by taking the approval of members by way of passing a special resolution in the General Meeting and by taking the approval of the Central Government on an application made in such form and manner as may be prescribed.

Step 1: Company to send notice to directors for convening Board meeting for approving items listed in step 2.

Step 2: Company to duly convene and held Board meeting as per section 173 and SS-1 for the approval of the below-mentioned items:

1. To consider the proposal of conversion of a public company into a private company;
2. To approve the amendment of articles of association of the company subject to the approval of members by way of General Meeting and Regional Director;
3. To authorize the director or any other eligible person on behalf of the company to do all acts as deemed necessary for giving effect to the proposal of conversion of a public company into a private company;
4. To authorize any practising professional to enter appearance before Regional Director for the aforesaid conversion;
5. To fix the date, time and venue of the General Meeting and authorize a director or company secretary to send the notice of the General Meeting to the members;

Step 3: Company to send notice to members as per section 101 and SS-2 for convening General Meeting for approving items by way of special resolution for items listed in step 4.

Step 4: Company to duly convene and conduct General meeting for approving the conversion of public company into a private company and thereby approving alteration in memorandum and articles of association of the Company under the provisions of Companies Act, 2013.

Step 5: Company to file e-form MGT-14 under section 117 of the Companies Act, 2013 within thirty (30) days of passing the special resolution along with the following documents as attachments:

1. Certified True Copy (CTC) of Special Resolution passed in General Meeting;
2. CTC of Notice along with Explanatory Statement to the Notice of Meeting;
3. CTC of altered Memorandum of Associations (MOA)
4. CTC of altered Articles of Associations (AOA)

Step 6: Drafting of Application for conversion of public limited company into a private limited company by setting out the following particulars as required under rule 41(2) of Companies (Incorporation) Rules, 2014, as amended:

1. The date of the Board meeting at which the proposal for alteration of Memorandum and Articles was approved;
2. The date of the general meeting at which the proposed alteration was approved;
3. Reason for conversion into a private company, the effect of such conversion on shareholders, creditors, debenture holders, deposit holders and other related parties;

Step 7: Preparation of List of Creditors: As per rule 41(3) of the Companies (Incorporation) Rules, 2014, as amended, there shall be attached to the application, a List of Creditors and Debenture Holders, drawn up to the latest practicable date preceding the date of filing of a petition by not more than 30 days, setting forth the following details, namely: -

1. The names and addresses of every creditor and debenture holder of the company;
2. The nature and respective amounts due to them in respect of debts, claims or liabilities;
3. In respect of any contingent or unascertained debt, the value, so far as can be justly estimated of such debt

Step 8: Advertisement of application in the Form INC. 25A at least 21 days before the date of filing of the application in:

1. Vernacular Newspaper in the principal vernacular language of the district in which the registered office of the company is situated; and
2. English language in an English Newspaper

(Widely circulated in the state in which the registered office of the company is situated)

Step 9: Notice to Creditors: The company shall at least 21 days before the date of filing of the application, by registered post with acknowledgement due, individual notice on every creditor and debenture holder of the Company.

Step 10: Notice to Regional Director, Registrar of Companies and other regulatory Body: The company shall ***at least 21 days*** before the date of filing of the application server, by registered post with acknowledgement due, a notice to the Regional Director and Registrar and the regulatory body, if the company is regulated under any law for the time being in force.

Step 11: Filling of Application with Registrar of Companies in **e-form GNL-1**: It is advisable to submit a copy of the application for conversion to the concerned ROC.

Step 12: Filling of Application for conversion with Regional Director in e-form RD-1: As per rule 41(1) of the Companies (Incorporation) Rules, 2014, as amended, an application for conversion of a public company into a private company shall be filed with Regional Director in e-form RD-1 within 60 days from the date of passing special resolution and shall be accompanied with following documents:

A draft copy of the Memorandum of Association and Articles of Association, with proposed alterations including the alterations under clause (68) of section 2;

A copy of the minutes of the general meeting at which the special resolution authorizing such alteration was passed together with details of votes cast in favour and or against with names of dissenters;

a copy of Board resolution or Power of Attorney dated not earlier than thirty days, as the case may be, authorizing to apply such conversion;

Step 13: The Regional Director will make an order approving the conversion on such terms and conditions if any, as it thinks fit.

Step 14: Obtain a certified copy of the order approving the conversion of a public company into a private company and file e-form INC-28 with the Registrar of Companies within 15 days from the date of receipt of approval.

Conversion of Private Company to Public Company

1. Calling of Board Meeting: Issue notice by the provisions of section 173(3) of the Companies Act, 2013, for convening a meeting of the Board of Directors.

The main agenda for this Board meeting would be:

a. Pass a board resolution to get in-principal approval of Directors for conversion of a private company into a public company by altering the AOA.

b. To approve notice of EGM along with Agenda and Explanatory Statement to be annexed to the notice of General Meeting as per section 102(1) of the Companies Act, 2013;

c. To authorize the Director or Company Secretary to issue Notice of the Extra-ordinary General meeting (EGM) as approved by the board under clause 1(c) mentioned above.

d. To consider and authorize any officer of the company to prepare the list of creditors and debenture holders, drawn up to the latest practicable date preceding the date of filing of application by a maximum of 30 days comprising of the following details:

2. Issue of EGM Notice: Issue Notice of the Extra-ordinary General meeting (EGM) to all Members, Directors and Auditors of the company by the provisions of Section 101 of the Companies Act, 2013;

3. Holding of Extra Ordinary General Meeting: Hold the Extra-ordinary General meeting (EGM) on the due date and pass the necessary Special Resolution, to get shareholders' approval for the Conversion of a Private Company into a Public company along with alteration in articles of association under section 14 for such conversion.

4. ROC Form filing: For alteration in Article of Association for conversion of Private Company into a Public company under section 14, a few E-forms will be filed with concerned Registrar of Companies at different stages as per the details given below:

a. E-form MGT.14 – For filing special resolution with ROC, passed for conversion of Private Company into a Public Company

- In case of alteration in Article of Association for conversion of Private Company into a Public Company Special resolution is required to be passed under section 14.
- Accordingly, as desired by section 117(3)(a), a copy of this special resolution is required to be filed with the concerned ROC through the filing of form MGT.14 within 30 days of passing the special resolution in the EGM.
- It is relevant to note that First you have to file form MGT.14 as SRN No. of form MGT.14 will be used in form INC.27.

Attachments of E-form MGT.14:

- i. Notice of EGM along with a copy of the explanatory statement under section 102;
- ii. Certified True copy of Special Resolution;
- iii. Altered memorandum of association;
- iv. Altered Articles of association
- v. Certified True copy of Board Resolution may be attached as an optional attachment.

E-form INC.27 – Application for conversion of a private company into a public company.

As per Rule 33 of Companies (Incorporation) Rules, 2014, for effecting the conversion of a private company into a public company or vice versa, the application shall be filed in Form No.INC-27 with fee.

Accordingly, an application for conversion of a Private company into a public company is required to be filed in e-Form INC.27 to the ROC concerned, with all the necessary annexures and with the prescribed fee.

i. It is mandatory to attach Minutes of the member's meeting where approval was given for conversion.

ii. Altered Articles of Association;

iii. Certified True copy of the Board Resolution may be attached as an optional attachment.

iv. Other information if any can be provided as an optional attachment(s)

Scrutiny of Documents by Roc:

- As per Section 18, after receiving the documents for conversion of a Private Company into a Public Company, ROC shall satisfy itself that the Company has complied with the requisite provisions for registration of the company.
- If so satisfied, ROC shall close the former registration and issue a fresh certificate of incorporation, after registering the documents submitted for change in class of company.

- It is further clarified in section 18(3) that conversion of the company does not affect any debts, liability, obligations or contracts incurred or entered into, by the company or on behalf of the company before conversion.
- Such debts, liabilities, obligations or contracts shall be enforceable in the same manner as if the such conversion has not been done.

Post Conversion Formalities:

- After the conversion of a Private Company into a Public Company kindly take care of the following points:
- Intimate all the concerned authorities like Excise and sales tax etc. about the status change.
- Arrange new PAN No. of the company. Update company bank account details.
- Arrange new stationery with the new name of the Company.
- Analyze your newly adopted AOA and MOA and remove all things which are in contradiction with the conditions of AOA.
- Raise the paid-up capital to a minimum of Rs. 5 lakhs, if the same is less than Rs. 5 lakhs
- Increase the Number of directors to a minimum of 3 Directors.

2.1.4 ON THE BASIS OF CONTROL

On the basis of control, companies may be classified into two categories:

1. Holding company [Sec. 4(4)].
2. Subsidiary company [Sec. 4(1)].

1. Holding Company:

According to Section 4(4) of the Companies Act, 1956 "A company shall be deemed to be the holding company of another, if that other is its subsidiary."

In some cases, a company's shares might be held fully or partly by another company. Here, the company owning these shares becomes the holding or parent company. Likewise, the company whose shares the parent company owns becomes its subsidiary company.

Holding companies exercise control over their subsidiaries by dictating the composition of their board of directors. Furthermore, parent companies also exercise control by owning more than 50% of their subsidiary companies' shares.

2. Subsidiary Company:

A company is said to be a subsidiary of another if:

(i) The other company controls the composition of its Board of Directors.

(ii) The other company holds more than half in nominal value of its equity share capital.

(iii) It is a subsidiary of such a company which is itself a subsidiary of any other company.

For example, if company B is the subsidiary of company A and company C is the subsidiary of company B then Company C also becomes the subsidiary of company A. If company D is the subsidiary of Company C, it also becomes a subsidiary of Company, A, A and so on.

2.1.5. ON THE BASIS OF OWNERSHIP

On the basis of ownership, the company may be a:

(i) Government company.

(ii) Non-government company.

1. Government Company:

According to section 617 of the Companies Act. 1956, Government company means, "any company in which not less than 51% of the paid-up share capital is held by the Central Government or by any State Government and includes a company which is a subsidiary of a Government Company." It may be a public company or a private company.

2. Non-Government Companies:

A non-Government company means a company which is not a government company. The majority of companies in India belong to this category.

2.17 Others

1. Foreign Company:

A foreign company means any company incorporated outside India but has established business in India.

These companies may be of the following two types:

(i) Companies incorporated outside India which established a place of business in India after the commencement of the Indian Companies Act, 1956; and

(ii) Companies incorporated outside India which established a place of business in India before the commencement of this Act and continued to have such a place of business in India at the time of commencement of this Act.

After the establishment of business in India, the following documents must be filed with the Registrar of Companies within 30 days from the date of establishment.

(i) A certified copy of the Memorandum and Articles of the company translated into English.

(ii) The complete address of the Registered Office of the company.

(iii) A list of directors and secretaries of the company.

(iv) The complete address of the place at which the company has constituted its main office in India.

2. One-Man Company:

A one-man company is a company where one man holds practically the whole of the share capital of the company and to meet the statutory requirement of the minimum number of members, some dummy names are added. The dummy names which are added are mostly the relatives or friends of the principal shareholder.

A one-man company is a legal entity distinct from its members. The company in law is equal to a natural person and has a legal entity of its own. The shareholder, even if he holds all the share is not a company. Neither he nor any creditor of the company has any property, legal or equitable, in the company's assets.

2.2 PRODUCER COMPANY

2.2.1 INTRODUCTION

With agriculture being the backbone of the Indian economy, the sector employs more than 50% of India's total workforce and contributes almost 17-18% to the country's GDP.

Considering the pressing issues of farmers and agriculturalists (collectively termed "Producers") in India, like agricultural labour, technological advancements, policy changes, etc., and to bring in better governance and channel agricultural activities, the concept of "Producer Company" was introduced in 2002. In this blog, we will further know what a producer company means, what are the registration procedures of a producer company, and the formation and benefits of a producer company.

2.2.2 DEFINITION OF PRODUCER COMPANY

Producer Company allows farmers' cooperatives to function as a corporate entity under the Ministry of Corporate Act.

According to the Companies Act 1956, the objective of the Producer Company is related to all or any of the following matters:

- Production
- Harvesting
- Procurement
- Grading
- Pooling
- Handling
- Marketing
- Selling
- Import/Export of primary produce

The Members of the Producer Company can carry out these activities by themselves or through other entities:

1. Processing, including preserving, drying, brewing, distilling, vinting, canning and packaging of produce
2. Manufacture or sale of equipment/machinery
3. Providing education on the mutual assistance principles to its Members and others
4. Offering technical services, consultancy services, training, R&D, and all other activities for the promotion of the interests of its Members
5. Generation, transmission and distribution of power, revitalization of land and water resources, their use, conservation and communications relatable to primary produce ;
6. Insurance of producers or their primary produce
7. Promoting techniques of mutuality and mutual assistance
8. Welfare measures or facilities for the benefit of Members as may be decided by the Board
9. Other activities that may promote the principles of mutuality and mutual assistance amongst the Members in any other manner
10. Financing of procurement, processing, marketing or other activities specified in clauses (a-j) which include extending of credit facilities or any other financial services to its Members

Every Producer Company shall deal primarily with the produce of its active Members for carrying out any of its objects specified in this section.

2.2.3 FORMATION AND PRODUCER COMPANY REGISTRATION

A Producer Company must be formed by:

- Ten or more individuals each of them being Producers; or by
- Two or more Producer institutions; or by
- A combination of 10 or more individuals and Producer institutions

The Producer Company must fulfil its objectives as specified in the Act.

The Registrar after being satisfied with the requirements will issue the Certificate of Incorporation within 30 days of receiving the necessary documents.

2.2.4 HOW TO REGISTER A PRODUCER COMPANY?

The procedure for a Producer Company registration is almost similar to that of a Private Limited Company.

Step 1:Obtain a Digital Signature Certificate (DSC) and Director's Identification Number (DIN) from all the Directors with self-attested copies of documents like PAN, Aadhaar card, and contact details.

Step 2:File the Proposed Company name in FORM-1A with the RoC of the respective state along with the prescribed fee. Once the name is available, the ROC informs about the availability of the name.

Step 3: Draft the Necessary Documents like MoA to incorporate the objects of the company and the amount of share capital to be registered, and AoA to contain the by-laws of the company.

Step 4: Filing of other Documents like Statutory declaration in Form-1 declaring compliance of all and incidental matters regarding the formation of companies; affidavit signed by the subscribers of the proposed company. Director's consent, utility bill, and NOC are required.

Step 5: The Certificate will be issued after which the Company shall become a corporate body as if it is a private limited company. Under any circumstances, it cannot become a public limited company.

2.2.5 MANAGEMENT OF PRODUCER COMPANY

Following are the important compliances a Producer Company is required to adhere to:

1. Every Producer Company shall have a minimum of five directors and a maximum of 15 directors.
2. The election for directors is to be conducted within 90 days of registering the company.
3. The Directors may be appointed or elected by the Members in the Annual General Meeting (AGM).
4. Every designated Director shall hold office for a minimum of one year and a maximum of 5 years as specified in the relevant articles.
5. AGM to be conducted once a year and shall be intimated through a notice specifying the meeting agenda, MoM (Minutes of Meeting), audited balance sheet, etc. The notice shall be sent not more than 15 months between the date of AGM and the next.
6. The first AGM should be conducted within 90 days from the date of incorporation.
7. The proceedings of every AGM along with the Director's Report audited balance sheet, P&L account and the annual returns shall be filed with the Registrar within 60 days of conducting the AGM.
8. If the Producer Company is formed by producer institutions, such institutions shall be represented in the general body through the Chairman of the Chief Executive
9. Proper books of accounts to be maintained concerning cash flow, expenditure, sales & purchase of goods, assets & liabilities, cost of labour, profit and loss statements, etc.
10. Internal Audit must be conducted by the Chartered Accountant at a specific interval and manner as specified in the Company's articles and per the Institute of Chartered Accountants Act, 1949.

2.2.6 BENEFITS OF REGISTERING A PRODUCER COMPANY

Producer Companies avail the following benefits:

- Every member of the Company will receive a value for the product or products pooled and supplied as determined by the Director. The amount will be distributed in cash or by allotment of equity shares. This may be subject to the conditions of the Board.

- Members can get bonus shares in proportion to the amount held.

- The additional amount that may be remaining after making provision for payment of limited return and reserves can be distributed as a patronage bonus. This will be in proportion to their participation in business activities either in cash or through equity shares.

- Members of Producer Company are also eligible to get financial assistance by way of a credit facility for a period not exceeding 6 months.
- Loans and advances against security as specified in articles, upon the condition of repayment within 3 months and not more than 7 years.

2.2.7 WHO CAN FORM A PRODUCER COMPANY?

Any 10 or more producers or individuals can join together to form a production company but there is no maximum limit on the number of members. Or, any 2 or more producer institutions can form a producer company. A minimum capital of Rs. 500,000 is required to incorporate a producer company.

2.2.8 WHAT IS A FARMER PRODUCER COMPANY?

A Farmer Producer Company can be formed by any 10 or more primary producers, by two or more producer institutions, or by a contribution of both. They can undertake activities related to production, harvesting, procurement, grading, pooling, marketing, processing, etc., of agricultural produce.

CHAPTER THREE

FORMATION OF COMPANY

Formation of Company - Preliminary Contracts – Certification of Incorporation Promotion - Certificate of Commencement of Business – MCA 21 – Scheme for Filing Statutory Documents and Other Transactions by Companies through Electronic Mode – Features of MCA 21.

3.1 INTRODUCTION

Company formation is the process of registering a business as a limited company at Companies House. As a result, the business becomes a distinct legal entity. The process is also referred to as 'company incorporation' and 'company registration'.

When incorporating a limited company, it becomes an individual 'person' in the eyes of the law. Incorporated businesses are completely separate from their owners in terms of finances, liabilities, contractual agreements, and ownership of property and assets. Such a view is not afforded to unincorporated businesses like sole traders as distinct legal entities.

A company is an artificial legal person that comes into existence by a process called "incorporation." It is only when a company has been incorporated, that it becomes a distinct entity from those who invested their capital as well as labour in it. Usually, for the formation of any company, the first step is the process known as "promotion" where a person persuades others to contribute capital to a proposed company before it is incorporated. Such a person is called the promoter of the company and its definition is given in Section 2(69) of the Companies Act, 2013.

Company Formation is the term for the business incorporation process in the UK. It is also sometimes referred to as **company registration**. These terms are both also used when incorporating a business in the Republic of Ireland. Under UK company law and most international law, a company or corporation is considered an entity that is separate from the people who own or operate the company.

Meaning

A company comes into existence when a group of people together with a view of forming an association to exploit the business opportunities by bringing material, money and management together.

Definition

Definition of a Company which can be formed under Section 3 of the Act

Before delving further into the details regarding the formation of a company, it is important to understand what exactly the meaning of these different types of companies is. **Section 2(68)** of the Act defines a private company as a company that has a minimum paid-up share capital as prescribed and restricts the right to transfer its shares according to the conditions laid down in the Articles of Association of the company. The maximum limit of members who can form a private company is 200 except in the case of an OPC.

Additionally, it is specified that for ascertaining the number of members, persons who jointly hold one or more shares shall be treated as a single member of the Act. The section also provides that employees of the company as well as a person who was a former employee as well as a member and who has ceased to be an employee but remains a member shall not be included for ascertaining the maximum number of members. Another feature of a private company is that it prohibits the public from subscribing to the shares of the company.

Based on the Minimum Number of Promoters in the Formation of a Company

Promoters are the persons who undertake the method of formation of a corporation. As per the Companies Act, 2013 (Section 3), depending upon the number of promoters meaning to form a company and other aspects, 3 types of companies can be formed as follows:

1. Public company (Minimum 7 Promoters/Persons)
2. Private company (Minimum 2 Promoters/Persons)
3. One Person Company (Minimum 1 Promoter/Person)

3.1.1 BASED ON THE CAPITAL STRUCTURE & COMPANY MAY BE REGISTERED AS SECTION 3 (2)

a. Company Limited by Shares:

In this company, capital is collected by issuing shares and therefore the liability of the members is limited to the extent of the unpaid part of the face value of shares bought by them.

b. Company Limited by Guarantee:

In this company, its members have bound to contribute a particular amount of cash either to the assets of the corporate at the time of completion or towards the value of winding up of the company.

c. Unlimited Liability Company:

In this company, the liability of its members is unlimited i.e. the members are liable to the whole amount of the company's debts and liabilities.

3.2 DETAILS CONCERNING THE FORMATION OF A COMPANY

Section 3 of the Act provides that in the form of a company, the members as prescribed above have to subscribe their names to the memorandum of the company and comply with the provisions of the Act. It is specifically provided that in the case of a one-person company, the memorandum has to indicate the name of the person with his prior consent in the prescribed form.

Such a person is to become a member of the company in the event of the subscriber's death or his incapacity to contract. Such a person's written consent has to be filed with the registrar at the time of incorporation of the One-person company along with his memorandum and articles.

It is also provided that such a person may withdraw his consent in the prescribed manner. Moreover, the member of the One-person company may also change the name of the nominee by following the prescribed procedure. A duty is vested upon the member to intimate the company of such in the nominee by indicating the same in the memorandum or otherwise. After this, the company has to notify the Registrar of Companies (RoC) of such change. This clarifies that such a change in a nominee is not to be treated as an alteration of the memorandum of the company.

3.2.1 MAIN REASONS FOR REJECTED COMPANY FORMATION

- The most common reasons a company formation is rejected are:
- A company name is unavailable, incomplete or missing from the application.
- A company name requires supporting evidence.

- Supporting evidence for a company name has been incorrectly presented.
- A company name contains a 'sensitive' word or expression.
- Incomplete details are provided for a director or company secretary.
- A residential address is flagged as being commercial property.
- Company share structure is incorrect.
- There is a problem with an officer's authentication.
- A company director does not meet the minimum age requirement of 16.
- A director is registered as an undischarged bankrupt or a disqualified director.
- A registered office address has not been included or is situated in the wrong country.
- The statement of capital is incomplete or missing.
- The articles of association have not been included.

3.3 STAGES OF FORMATION OF A COMPANY

There are four stages

1. Promotion Stage

2. Incorporation or Registration Stage

3. Capital Subscription Stage

4. Commencement of Business Stage

The Companies Act, 2013; Section 3(1) has stated the following conditions for the formation of a company:

i) a Corporation Shall be Formed for Any Lawful Purpose.

ii) Minimum 7 promoters needed for a public company, minimum 2 promoters for the personal company and 1 promoter for One Person Company

iii) All the promoters must subscribe their names to the Memorandum of Association.

iv) The promoters must comply with all the provisions of the Companies Act, 2013 concerning the incorporation of a company.

Stage: 1 Promotion Stage:

Promotion is the first stage in the formation of a company. The term 'Promotion' refers to the aggregate of activities designed to bring into being an enterprise to operate a business. It presupposes the technical processing of a commercial proposition concerning its potential profitability. The meaning of promotion and the steps to be taken in promoting a business are discussed in brief here.

Promotion of a company refers to the total activities of all those who participate in the building of the enterprise up to the organization of the company and completion of the plan to exploit the idea. It begins with serious consideration given to the ideas on which the business is to be based. In other words

Definition:

According to C.W. Grestembeg, "Promotion may be defined as the discovery of business opportunities and the subsequent organization of funds, property and managerial ability into a business concern to make profits therefrom."

According to H.E. Heagland, "Promotion is the process of creating a specific business enterprise. Its scope is very broad, and numerous individuals are frequently asked to make their contributions to the programme. Promotion begins when someone gives serious consideration to the formulation of the ideas upon which the business in question is to be based. When the corporation is organized and ready for operation, the major function of promotion comes to an end."

Stages of Promotion

The promotion stage includes various stages to fulfil the desired results of the first stage

1. **Identification of Business Opportunity:**

The first stage in the promotion of a business is the identification of a business opportunity. The promoter visualizes that there are opportunities for a particular type of business and it can be run profitability. The idea may be to exploit a new area of natural resources or a venture in the existing line of business. He develops ideas with the help of technical experts in that field. When the promoter feels that there are opportunities in taking up a particular venture then the idea is taken further.

1. **Detailed Investigation:**

In the second stage, various factors relating to the business are studied from a practical point of view. The demand for the product is estimated and the likely business share is determined. After determining the prospective demand, the promoter thinks of arranging finances, labour, raw materials, power, etc. The cost structure of the product is analyzed to find out the profitability of the venture. An expert opinion is sought upon the viability of the project.

3. **Approval of Name:**

It is necessary to get the name of the company approved by the Registrar of Companies. This is done to avoid duplication of the name. Generally, a company submits a list of names in order of preference. The Registrar matches the names with the names of existing companies and then one name is approved.

4. **Signatories to Memorandum:**

The promoters decide the names of persons to be the signatories to the memorandum of association. Usually, the first signatories to the memorandum become the first directors of the company. The written consent of the persons to act as directors is taken and they are asked to take qualifying shares of the company.

5. **Appointment of Professionals:**

The next stage is of raising funds and deciding about various contracts. So, promoters appoint brokers and underwriters to ensure the availability of capital by the sale of the company's securities. They also appoint solicitors to deal with legal matters of the company.

6. **Preparing necessary Documents:**

The promoters take steps to prepare various legal documents for the company which have to be submitted to the Registrar of Companies at the time of incorporation. The documents which are required to be prepared include Memorandum of Association, Articles of Association, Prospectus, etc.

Who is a Promoter in a Company?

A successful promoter is a creator of wealth and an economic prophet. The person who is concerned with the promotion of a business enterprise is known as the Promoter. He conceives the idea of starting a business and takes all the measures required for bringing the enterprise into existence.

For example, Dhirubhai Ambani is the promoter of Reliance Industries.

The promoters find out the ways to collect money, investigate business ideas arrange for finance, assemble resources and establish a going concern.

The company law has not given any legal status to promoters. He stands in a fiduciary position.

Types of Promoters

Promoters are different types such as professional promoters, occasional promoters, promoter companies, financial promoters, entrepreneurs, lawyers and engineers.

Professional Promoters: These are the persons who specialize in the promotion of companies. They hand over the companies to shareholders when the business starts. In India, there is a lack of professional promoters. In many other countries, professional promoters have played an important role and helped the business community to a great extent. In England, Issue Houses; In the U.S.A., Investment Banks and in Germany, Joint Stock Banks have played the role of promoters very appreciably.

Occasional Promoters: These promoters take interest in floating some companies. They are not in promotion work regularly but take up the promotion of some company and then go to their earlier profession. For instance, engineers, lawyers, etc. may float some companies.

Financial Promoters: Some financial institutions of financiers may take up the promotion of a company. They generally take up this work when the financial environment is favourable at the time.

Managing Agents as Promoters: In India, Managing Agents played an important role in promoting new companies. These persons used to float new companies and then got their Managing Agency rights. The Managing Agency system has since long been abolished in India.

Legal Position of Promoter: The company law has not given any legal status to promoters. A promoter is neither an agent nor a trustee of the company because it is a non-entity before incorporation. Some legal cases have tried to specify the status of a promoter. He stands in a fiduciary position.

The promoter moulds and creates the company and under his supervision it comes into existence. The promoter must get maximum benefits for the company. He should not get secret profits from the company. If he sells his property to the company, then he should explain his interest in such property.

Liabilities of a Promoter

Following are the liabilities of a promoter

- A promoter should not make secret profits out of the dealings of the company.
- (ii) He must deposit with the company all money received on its behalf.
- (Hi) He must exercise due diligence and care while performing the work of a promoter.
- (iv)He will be personally responsible for all the preliminary contracts till all these are approved by the company.
- (v) He will compensate any person who made investments in the company based on untrue statements made by the promoter.

Stage: 2 Incorporation or Registration Stage:

Incorporation or registration is the second stage in the formation of a company. It is the registration that brings a company into existence. A company is properly constituted only when it is duly registered under the Act and a Certificate of Incorporation has been obtained from the Registrar of Companies.

Procedure to Get a Company Registered

To get a company registered or incorporated, the following procedure is to be adopted:

(A) Preliminary Activities:

Before a company is incorporated, the promoter has to decide the following:

1. To decide the name of the company
2. License under Industries Development and Regulation Act, 1951

(B) Filing of Document with the Registrar:

1. Memorandum of Association
2. Articles of Association
3. List of directors
4. Written consent of directors
5. Statutory declaration

To get the company registered, the important documents required to be filed with the Registrar of Companies are as follows.

1. **Memorandum of Association:** It is to be signed by a minimum of 7 persons for a public company and by 2 in the case of a Pvt company. It must be properly stamped.

2. **Articles of Association:** This document is signed by all those persons who have signed the Memorandum of Association.

3. **List of Directors:** A list of directors with their names, address and occupation is to be prepared and filed with the Registrar of Companies.

4. **Written consent of the Directors:** A written consent of the directors that they have agreed to act as directors has to be filed with the Registrar along with a written undertaking to the effect that they will take qualification shares and will pay for them.

5. **Notice of the Address of the Registered Office:** It is also customary to file the notice of the address of the company's registered office at the time of incorporation. It is to be given within 30 days after the date of incorporation.

6. **Statutory Declaration:** A statutory declaration by

a. any advocate of the Supreme Court or
b. of a High Court, or
c. an attorney or pleader entitled to appear before a High Court or
d. a practising chartered accountant in India, who engages in the Company formation or
e. by a person indicated in the articles as director, managing director, Secretary or manager of the company, mentioning that the requisites of the Act and the rules there under have been complied with. It is to be filed with the Registrar of Companies.

When the required documents have been filed with the Registrar along with the prescribed fee, the Registrar scrutinizes the documents. If the Registrar is satisfied, the name of the company is entered into the register. Then the Registrar issues a certificate known as a Certificate of Incorporation.

3.4 PRELIMINARY CONTRACTS

Meaning

A pre-incorporation contract is an agreement that is made by a person at the behest of a company or corporation that does not exist at the time of signing such an agreement. These agreements are entered into as there are preliminary contracts and expenses incurred before an organization takes form. An example of a pre-incorporation contract is a co-founders' agreement. The person who is signing the agreement on behalf of the company intends to bind the company to the agreement in future when the company is finally incorporated.

The person who enters into a pre-incorporation agreement is usually called the Promoter. The Indian Companies Act 2013 (hereinafter "**the Companies Act**") defines the Promoter under *Section 2(69)* as a person who has been (a) named in the prospectus, (b) who has control over the affairs of the company, and (c) according to whose directions the Board of Directors acts. But this definition only defines the Promoter once the company has been formed and not before its incorporation.

3.4.1 LEGAL STATUS OF PRE-INCORPORATION CONTRACTS IN INDIA

The legal status of pre-incorporation contracts is not easy to define. According to the Indian Contract Act 1872 (hereinafter "**the Contract Act**"), all agreements are contracts if they are made with the free consent of the parties who are competent to contract for lawful consideration. However, during the pre-incorporation stage, the company on whose behalf the Promoter is agreeing does not exist. Hence, a company cannot enter into a contract before its existence.

It can only sign an agreement after its name is registered with the Registrar of Companies by the Companies Act. Furthermore, the Promoters are acting as "agents" of the company while entering into these pre-incorporation contracts. However, if the principal i.e. if the existence of the company itself is not an actuality how can the Promoter nominate herself as an agent of the company? Hence, the Promoters themselves become personally liable for all agreements entered by them on behalf of the company, even though they claim to have entered into contracts for the benefit of the company.

Under Section 230 of the Contract Act, an agent cannot personally enforce or bind the principal on her behalf. In the present case, the principal i.e. the company does not exist, thus she cannot bind the company by an agreement. Similarly, if the Promoter is acting as an agent of the principal company, she cannot be personally held liable for breach of contract. If this principle is followed, the contract becomes unenforceable as neither principal (to be incorporated company) nor the agent (the Promoter) can be held liable for breach of contract. Here is where the Indian Specific Relief Act of 1963 (hereinafter "**the Specific Relief Act**") comes to the affected party's rescue.

3.4.2 MAKING THEM ENFORCEABLE IN INDIA

According to Section 15(h) of the Specific Relief Act, specific performance of a contract can be obtained by any party thereto or a representative in the interest of the principal, when the Promoters of a company have entered into a contract before the incorporation of a company and such a contract is warranted under the company's incorporation terms. Similarly, under Section 19(e) of the Specific Relief Act if the newly incorporated company has accepted the pre-incorporation contract and has communicated its acceptance to the other party, relief against parties can be claimed under the subsequent title.

Therefore, pre-incorporation contracts can be enforced in India by (i) incorporating the contract in the terms of incorporation, (b) by entering into a new contract with the other party or the Promoter, and (c) by expressly or impliedly accepting the benefits of the pre-incorporation contract.

3.4.4INSTRUCTIONS FOR DRAFTING PRE-INCORPORATION CONTRACTS

Any pre-incorporation contract must have the following items:

Shareholders' Name: The shareholders' names including the names of the promoters in the future company must be mentioned.

Incorporation: The State in which the company would be incorporated must be mentioned. Although the Companies Act is a central legislation and would govern all the companies incorporated under it; incorporating it in certain States can have some advantages. Such benefits can include having courts in the State jurisdiction that support corporate businesses as opposed to State courts that do not. Some States can be communistic and not support policies that would help capitalistic trade and businesses such as Kerala and West Bengal.

An ideal place of incorporation would be the State where the future company would conduct its business with other corporations. It is good to attach a draft copy of the Articles of Association and Memorandum of Association with the pre-incorporation agreement.

Corporate Name: The name of the future company must be added to the pre-incorporation agreement. It is important to ensure that the name of the company is available. For this, the Ministry of Corporate Affairs website can be used to search for already registered company names.

Corporate Address: The corporate address that would be mentioned in the Articles of Association and Memorandum of Association must be written in the pre-incorporation agreement.

Name of the Proposed Directors: Any Director chosen or proposed Director must be stated in the agreement signed before the company's incorporation.

Capital Contribution: The capital contribution of the subscribers and the mode in which they would contribute must be added to the pre-incorporation agreement.

Opening of Bank Account: Every company must open a corporate bank account for its income and expenditure. In which bank will the future company open its corporate account and who would be the authorized person(s) to transact on behalf of the company must all be stated in the pre-incorporation agreement.

Corporate Purpose: The purpose of the company would have to be inserted in the pre-incorporation agreement. Simple language must be used, and the purpose must be broad enough to cover all the intended purposes and possible activities of the future company.

Samples:

1. To operate one or more retail stores for the sale of computer equipment.
2. To manufacture and distribute equipment for preparing cappuccino.
3. To design websites for law firms.
4. To cater parties, weddings, and other events requiring food services, and decoration, and to rent equipment to be used in connection with these services.

Due Date: A target date by which time the company would be duly registered and incorporated with the Registrar of Companies must also be mentioned in the pre-incorporation agreement

Corporate Stock: The total number of shares the corporation will be issuing to the shareholders who would sign the pre-incorporation agreement must be mentioned. One must not forget the difference between authorized stock and issued stock. Authorized stock is the maximum number of shares a company can issue, whereas the issued stock is what the company has announced. It also must be stated that the shares issued would be common stock i.e. it would not be assured that some kind of dividend or profit would be paid on those shares.

Reimbursement of Expenses: If a shareholder is handling all the responsibilities for the incorporation of the company and its corporate matters, such a shareholder must be reimbursed for her fees and expenditure. Such reimbursement must also be covered under the agreement.

General Boilerplate Clauses: Standard contractual clauses such as dispute resolution, the jurisdiction of courts, confidentiality, damages to be paid, termination of the agreement, method of incorporating or enforcing the agreement after the company has been registered and incorporated, etc. must also be included in the pre-incorporation agreement.

3.5 CERTIFICATE OF INCORPORATION

A certificate of incorporation is a legal document required at the time of company formation. It is said to be a license to form a company, issued by the state government. The private limited company in India is measured by the shares that a shareholder is only liable to a limit of creditors.

On the registration of the memorandum and other documents, the Registrar will issue a certificate known as the Certificate of Incorporation certifying under his hand that the company is incorporated and, in the case of a limited company that the company is limited. A Certificate of Incorporation (or Letter of Incorporation) is a legal document that is issued by the Ministry of Corporate Affairs to a company in India once they are successfully registered with them. This certificate is proof that the company is registered with the Registrar of Companies.

A Pvt. limited company cannot offer their share to the general public, so it cannot trade on the public stock exchanges, the main difference between a Private limited and a public limited company.

The private limited company has to suffix limited or incorporation as the name is the reason of lid or inc written at the end of the company name.

Registration as a private limited company certificate of incorporation is the last step, which is mailed after the approval of all documents required for the **company formation.**

3.5.1 PRIVATE COMPANY REGISTRATION OR COMPANY FORMATION

- Filling applications for **DIN** and DSC that are Director Identification Number and Digital Signature Certificate
- Selecting and checking and then applying for the availability of the name selected
- Drafting of MOA and AOA that are Memorandum of association and article of the association respectively
- Filling of E-forms with Registrar of companies
- Registrar of companies' fees and stamp duty have to be paid for it.
- All verification of the documents/forms by Registrar of companies
- After all these, a Certificate of Incorporation is issued to the director of the company

3.5.2 PROCESS OF ISSUING A CERTIFICATE OF INCORPORATION

A certificate of Incorporation is the legal document which makes the company formation valid or brings the company into existence. Certificate of Incorporation mainly includes five things in it

- The name of the corporation with its abbreviation
- A statement of business purposes corporation's registered office's address and the name of the registered agent for the address
- Number of the shares of stock which are authorized to be issued and a description of the different types of stock that can be issued by the Company if there are more than one type
- The name and address of the corporation incorporated
- Certificate of incorporation has been divided into different articles but many other things can be included in the certificate of Incorporation. There should be a **digital signature** which should add by the director of the corporation. For more information,

3.5.3 HOW TO OBTAIN A COPY OF A CERTIFICATE OF INCORPORATION?

- A certificate of incorporation lists the organizational details of a corporation, including its structure and the names of its officers. This is all public information, so anyone can request a copy of any company's certificate of incorporation.
- The corporation's registered office's address and the name of the registered agent for the address
- Number of the shares of stock which are authorized to be issued and a description of the different types of stock that can be issued by the Company if there are more than one type
- The name and address of the corporation incorporated

Secretary of State's Website:

- A certificate of incorporation lists the organizational details of a corporation, including its structure and the names of its officers. This is all public information, so anyone can request a copy of any company's certificate of incorporation.
- Each state has its procedure for requests, with some offering online ordering, while others require you to mail in a written form. You must also pay a fee for processing and photocopying, which may vary based on the size of the document.

Search Your Business Name:

- Look for a link titled "Corporate Filings" or "Business Entities" on the state's website. Click the link to bring up the business entity search screen. Type the company name in the search box and press "Enter" or click the "Search" button.
- Look through the search results and click the link for your company to display any available details. Select your company and confirm the details are correct. Be aware that some companies have similar names so be sure to select the correct one.

Complete Request Forms:

- Fill out the online order form to request a copy of the certificate of incorporation, if your state offers one to order business documents. If you are not able to request a copy online, the site should have a form you can download and print out. Fill out the required information, and sign and date the form. Mail it to the address listed on the state's website.

Pay Processing Fee:

- Note any fees that may be associated with the replacement paperwork. Every state is different. Pay the processing fee according to the fee schedule on the website. If you were able to place your order online, you will probably also be able to make a payment online. If this option is not available, find a mailing address for payments on the website.
- Write a check or purchase a money order for the required amount and mail it to the listed address. Generally, you will include the check with a paper form mailed to the secretary of state.

3.5.4 IMPORTANCE OF CERTIFICATE OF INCORPORATION

- Any type of business needs to go through the process of incorporation. This process involves preparing specific documents, including the Articles of Incorporation, and filing documents with the secretary of state. For limited liability companies (LLCs), the main documents used to incorporate are the Articles of Organization.
- **Shields From Liability**. If you operate an unincorporated business, creditors might reach your assets. Your residence and personal bank account might pay down debts or satisfy lawsuits against your business. When you incorporate, the business and all of its owners remain separate entities.
- **Establishes Perpetual Existence and Transfer of Ownership**. Perpetual existence means the business remains unaffected by the withdrawal or death of one of the owners. Similarly, an unincorporated business is difficult to transfer ownership. If the business is incorporated, shareholders can transfer their interest by gift or sale.

- **Gains Tax Advantages.** Incorporated business gain tax deductions for operating costs, which lower your company's tax liability.
- These deductions may include employee wages, insurance costs, retirement plan costs, and material/production costs.
- **Enhances the Company's Image.** Incorporating your business adds credibility, particularly if your company has Incorporated, Company, or Limited (or any of its abbreviations) after its name. Customers are more likely to trust a business that has a positive image. It also makes the company more attractive to banks and investors if it needs outside financing.
- **Improves Ability to Manage.** An incorporated business has shareholders involved with the board of directors. The board delegates the authority to the company's officers. An unincorporated business could have a co-owner or employee who holds all the power and decision-making authority. This lack of structure can adversely affect the company.

3.5.5 IMPORTANT DOCUMENTS NECESSARY FOR FORMING OF A COMPANY

When it comes to forming your company, you must take note of the important documents you need:

Certificate of Incorporation. This legal document is necessary when forming a company or corporation. The state government or non-governmental entity issues the license to form the corporation. It essentially serves as the birth certificate of your company.

Certificate of Commencement. The date of incorporation cannot be the same date of commencement of business (COB). At the point of commencement, a public or private limited company that doesn't have shared capital does not need to comply with any other legal formalities.

Companies commence business activities immediately after securing the Certificate of Incorporation. Public and private limited companies that share capital must obtain a Certificate of Commencement of business before they can commence the business or borrow money.

3.5.6 CERTIFICATE OF INCORPORATION AND A BUSINESS BANK ACCOUNT

- When opening a business bank account, the Certificate of Incorporation is one of the most important documents you need to bring with you. This document shows that you have set up your business correctly. In addition, it shows that the business is a legal entity and is on the public register of companies.
- Banks must comply with strict regulations and rules, particularly when it comes to money laundering.
- That's why you must bring identification with you as well as documents about your company's formation.
- Other important documents you must bring, including the Certificate of Incorporation, include the memorandum, Articles of Incorporation, and any issued share certificates.

Effects of Incorporation

The certificate of incorporation is conclusive evidence of the fact that:

(i) The company is properly incorporated and duly registered;

(ii) The terms of the Memorandum and Articles are within the law;

(iii) All requirements of the Act in respect of registration have been complied with;

(iv) A private company can start its business after getting the certificate of incorporation; and

(v) With the issue of the certificate, the company takes birth with a separate legal entity.

For this purpose, soon after the incorporation, a meeting of the Board of Directors is convened to deal with the following business:

1. Appointment of the Secretary. In most cases, the appointment of the pre-tem secretary (who is appointed at the promotion stage) is confirmed.

2. Appointment of bankers, auditors, solicitors and brokers etc.

3. Adoption of draft 'prospectus' or 'statement instead of a prospectus.

4. Adoption of underwriting contract, if any.

Besides the above-mentioned business, the Board also decides as to whether:

(i) a public offer for capital subscription is to be made, and

(ii) Listing of shares at a stock exchange is to be secured.

The company will now proceed to obtain the permission of the Controller of Capital Issue, New Delhi, under the Capital Issue Control Act, 1947 if a public offer for the sale of shares and debentures exceeding Rs. one crore is to be made during 12 months unless the issue fulfils the conditions of exemption as laid down in the Capital Issue (Exemption) Order, 1969.

The Capital Issue Control Act, 1947 however, does not apply to a private company, a banking company, an insurance company, or a government company provided it does not make an issue of securities to the general public.

After the above formalities have been completed, the directors of the company file a copy of the 'prospectuses with the Registrar and invite the public to subscribe to the shares of the company by putting the 'prospectus' in circulation.

Application for shares are received from the public through the company's bankers and if the subscribed capital is at least equal to the minimum subscription amount as disclosed in the prospectus, and other conditions of a valid allotment are fulfilled, the directors of the company pass a formal resolution of allotment.

Allotment letters are then posted, a return of allotment is filed with the Registrar and share certificates are issued to the allotters in exchange for the allotment letters. If the subscribed capital is less than the minimum subscription or the company could not obtain the minimum subscription within 120 days of the issue of the prospectus, all money will be refunded and no allotment can be made.

It may be noted that a public company having a share capital, but not issuing a 'prospectus' has to file with the Registrar a Statement instead of a Prospectus' at least three days before the directors proceed to pass the first allotment resolution.

3.5.7 Who Needs to Submit a Certificate of Incorporation?

Entrepreneurs who want to operate their company as a corporation a legal entity that is separate from and that provides personal liability protection for its owners must file a certificate of incorporation form.

They must have their certificate of incorporation approved by the state (usually the Secretary of State Office) before they can conduct certain activities in the business name. Some examples include:

- Open a corporate bank account
- Apply for business licenses and permits
- Hire employees
- File taxes

3.5.8 WHEN IS THE BEST TIME TO FILE FOR INCORPORATION?

As I mentioned, a business will need its certificate of incorporation to carry out some key activities under its business name. So a good time to file a certificate of incorporation paperwork is generally after business owners have decided that they want to operate their company as a corporation after they have conducted corporate name and trademark searches to make sure that the name they want to use is available, and after they have secured a registered agent.

Perhaps you're wondering what time of year is ideal for incorporating. That depends. Business owners can submit the paperwork at any time. If launching the business as soon as possible is the goal, it's important to know how long it might take the state to process the request. Most state websites provide an estimate of how long the wait might be. Existing businesses that want to switch from some other structure to a corporation might consider making the change effective on January 1 of the new year. That allows for a clean break from operating as one structure in the past year to operating as a corporation in the next year, thus eliminating the need to file two sets of tax forms as would happen with a mid-year switch.

3.5.9 WHAT INFORMATION DOES A CERTIFICATE OF INCORPORATION INCLUDE?

The information requested on the certificate of incorporation form may vary slightly from one state to the next. I've listed some of the details you might be expected to share below:

Type of corporation being registered. Some examples include:

- Business stock
- Business nonstock
- Business-statutory close
- Management
- Professional
- Insurance
- Nonprofit
- Benefit
- Cooperative

3.5.10 HOW MUCH DOES IT COST TO FILE FOR A CERTIFICATE OF INCORPORATION?

Just as the information a state requires may be different from what another state asks for, the fees to file for a certificate of incorporation can vary, too. The filing fee might be a flat fee that applies to all corporations, or it might depend on the number of authorized shares the corporation will have or a combination of the two. To find out what the fee in your state is, I suggest visiting your state's Secretary of State Office website to find that information.

Note that the certificate of the incorporation filing fee is just one of the costs entrepreneurs must plan for when forming a corporation. Other legal and government filing fees might include:

- **State franchise tax** – For the privilege of doing business as a corporation in the state
- **Business licenses and permits** – Depending on the type of business and where it's located
- **Attorney's fees** – For legal guidance and handling legal documents

3.6 SCHEME FOR FILING STATUTORY DOCUMENTS AND OTHER TRANSACTIONS BY COMPANIES THROUGH ELECTRONIC MODE

Under the newly introduced **Companies (Amendment) Ordinance 2018**, all companies registered in India after the commencement of the **Companies (Amendment) Ordinance, 2018** and having a share capital is required to obtain a **commencement of business** certificate before commencing any business or exercising any borrowing powers. Since The Companies (Amendment) Ordinance 2018 was introduced on November 2nd 2018, any company incorporated after November 2018 would be required to obtain a Commencement of Business Certificate.

'Commencement of Business' this concept was there in the erstwhile Companies Act, 1956 and it was also introduced by the Companies Act, 2013 under Section 11 of the **Companies Act, 2013**. However, section 11 was omitted (deleted) LATER ON by the companies (Amendment) Act, 2015 w.e.f. 29th May 2015.

Declaration for **Commencement of business** is re-introduced by way of inserting a new Section 10A after section 10 of the Companies Act, 2013. The DETAIL of Section 10A is as follow;

Extract of Section 10A. Commencement of business etc.

(1) A company incorporated after the commencement of the ***Companies (Amendment) Ordinance, 2018*** *and having a share capital shall not commence any business or exercise any borrowing powers unless—*

(a) a declaration is filed by a director within a period of one hundred and eighty days of the date of incorporation of the company in such form and verified in such manner as may be prescribed, with the Registrar that every subscriber to the memorandum has paid the value of the shares agreed to be taken by him on the date of making of such declaration; and

(b) The company has filed with the Registrar a verification of its registered office as provided in sub-section (2) of section 12.

(2) If any default is made in complying with the requirements of this section, the company shall be liable to a penalty of fifty thousand rupees and every officer who is in default shall be liable to a penalty of one thousand rupees for each day during which such default continues but not exceeding the number of one lakh rupees.

(3) Where no declaration has been filed with the Registrar under clause (a) of sub-section (1) within a period of one hundred and eighty days of the date of incorporation of the company and the Registrar has reasonable cause to believe that the company is not carrying on any business or operations, he may, without prejudice to the provisions of sub-section (2), initiate action for the removal of the name of the company from the register of companies under Chapter XVIII.]].

3.6.1 MANDATORY TO OBTAIN A CERTIFICATE OF COMMENCEMENT OF BUSINESS FOR REGISTERED COMPANIES:

Companies registered on or after November 02, 2018, are required to file the declaration for commencement of business with the Registrar of companies

Time limit:*

The declaration for **commencement of business** shall be filed within 180 days from the date of getting the CERTIFICATE OF INCORPORATION. The ordinance came into force on 2nd Nov 2018 therefore all the provisions of this section become applicable from 2nd November 2018. Therefore, every company having share capital incorporated after 2nd November 2018 has to file form 20A within 180 days i.e., before 1st May 2019. The Ministry of Corporate Affairs has launched form 20A and it's available on its portal.

3.6.2 CERTIFICATION OF FORM 20A

This e-form 20A needs to be verified by practising professional i,e, (Company Secretary) CS /(Chartered Accountant) CA/ (Cost accountant) CWA. For any negligence or default in certification, practising professionals shall be liable to face the consequences as per the PROVISION of sections 448 and 449 of the Companies Act, 2013.

3.6.3 VERIFICATION OF REGISTERED OFFICE – SEC-12(2)

Declaration in E-form INC-20A by a director, also states a point i.e. point no – 4 that "The company has filed with the registrar a verification of its registered office as provided in subsection (2) of section 12", now the question is who is required to file this verification with the registrar of companies and by what period?

While the **incorporation of the company**, in company incorporation form SPICE – INC-32, if you have selected the option "No" in point 4(b) i.e. whether the address for correspondence is the address of the registered office of the company, then you need to file verification of registered office with the registrar of companies within 30 days from the date of incorporation of the company.

3.6.4 VERIFICATION SHALL BE FILED IN E-FROM INC-22 WITHIN 30 DAYS FROM THE DATE OF INCORPORATION

Attachments of E-form INC-22: –

(a) Proof of registered office – Rent Agreement/Lease agreement or Conveyance agreement

(b) Copy of Utility Bill (not older than two months) – Electricity Bill/Water Bill/Telephone Bill (anyone)

(c) A proof that the Company is permitted to use the address as the registered office of the Company if the same is owned by any other entity/ Person – NOC from the owner of the premises (in case of rented premises)

(d) List of all the companies (specifying their CIN) having the same registered office address, if any

3.6.5 SCHEME FOR FILING OF STATUTORY DOCUMENTS

In exercise of the powers conferred by sub-section (2) of section 610B of the Companies Act, 1956 (1 of 1956) the Central Government has decided to make a Scheme for implementation of the e-Governance Programme named as "MCA-21 Project" to give effect to the provision of sub-section (1) of section 610B to provide corporate and other entities and individuals, easy and secure online services including the filing of statutory data and registration throughout the country and to enable companies to carry out various transactions with the offices of the Registrars of Companies, Regional Directors and the Central Government in the electronic mode. The Central Government hereby makes the scheme for implementation and administration of the e-Governance programme as follows:—

Short Title and Commencement

1. (1) The Scheme shall be known as the "Scheme for Filing of Statutory Documents and other Transactions by Companies in Electronic Mode".

   (2) This Scheme shall be applicable from the date of its publication in the Official Gazette.

   The Scheme

2. The Scheme for Filing Statutory Documents and other Transactions by Companies in Electronic Mode is in Annexure 'A'.

Application of the Information Technology Act, 2000 (21 of 2000)

3. The Scheme would operate under the provisions of the Companies Act, 1956, and insofar as the provisions for use of Information Technology are not specifically made under the Companies Act, 1956, the provisions contained in the Information Technology Act, 2000 will apply.

   Saving

4. The transactions filed in the electronic mode and processed under the launch of the first pilot project for e-Governance, *i.e.,* MCA21, at Coimbatore with effect from 18- 2-2006 and subsequent operationalization of the project at different locations till the date of notification of the Scheme shall be deemed to have been filed and processed under the provisions of this Scheme.

ANNEXURE 'A'

Scheme For Filing of Statutory Documents and Other Transactions By Companies In Electronic Mode

Background

1. (1) MCA-21 is one of the mission mode projects of the Government of India under the National e-Governance plan to provide easy and secure online services through the use of information technology to various stakeholders in the corporate sector in the country.

2. The "MCA-21 Project" was initially launched at Coimbatore as a Pilot Project on 18-2- 2006. The second Pilot was launched in Delhi on 18-3-2006 by the Hon'ble Prime.

Minister of India. Thereafter, the project was launched progressively and the nationwide roll-out has been completed across all Registrars of Companies (RoC) jurisdictions. The MCA-21 e-Governance Project is the first of its kind for the Government of India. A programme of this size and magnitude, being comprehensive and complex, is bound to face transitional problems in the initial stages after the roll-out on the ground. As such, it has been found necessary to provide for a stabilization period of one year for the programme till 31-3-2007.

3. (*i*) The e-Governance programme has been implemented following the BOOT (Build, Own, Operate and Transfer) framework. The project consists of the period required for implementation till the roll-out stage at all sites with testing and certification, and the operation period of six years over which payments towards project cost in the form of fixed equated quarterly instalments would be made to the BOOT Operator by the project owner. The BOOT Operator is responsible for:

a. designing and implementing the project till the stage of roll-out at all sites with testing and certification thereof;
b. owning, operating and maintaining the system for six years after successful roll-out at all sites;
c. undertaking necessary replacement investments at the end of the third year/beginning of the fourth year,

(*ii*) M/s. TCS-CMC consortium was selected as the BOOT Operator following an open competitive bidding process. The implementation of the project started on 1-3-2005.

4. With the enactment of the Companies (Amendment) Act, 2006 (No. 23 of 2006), published in the Gazette of India (Extraordinary), dated 30-5-2006 the Companies Act, 1956, provides under section 610B of the Act, a comprehensive statutory framework for enabling electronic filing, storage, retrieval, viewing, processing and transmission of company data required to be filed with the Registrar of Companies under the Companies Act, 1956. The Central Government may appoint different dates in respect of different RoCs or Regional Directors from which such scheme shall come into force.
5. Since the processing of company documents submitted in the electronic form would also be carried out electronically, it is envisaged that filing of all statutory forms, their processing, approvals and responses by the RoCs thereon would also be in electronic mode.

The Scheme

The Scheme for Filing of statutory Documents and other Transactions by Companies in Electronic Mode relates to the electronic filing, storage, retrieval viewing, processing and transmission of company data required to be filed with the Registrars of Companies, Regional Directors and Central Government under the Companies Act, 1956.

Transactions covered under the Scheme

(1) The transactions covered under the e-Governance programme are as under:—

a. Incorporation of Company

b. Filing of all annual statutory returns
c. Registration, modification and satisfaction of charges
d. Statutory filings related to all events as stipulated in the Companies Act (except matters related to liquidation)
e. Inspection of documents
f. Issue of certified copies
g. Approvals from Regional Director
h. Approvals from the Central Government
a. Investor complaints:

Provided that the scheme would not apply to matters about the liquidation of companies.

While some of the transactions could involve the submission of physical papers due to various requirements such as stamp duty, signed copy of the complaint by the complainant, provision of supporting documents, issue of certified copies of documents, etc.; the objective in the long-term remains to process of all transactions in a complete electronic mode.

Issuance of certificates and such other approvals will continue to remain on paper and, as a general rule, will be dispatched by post/courier to the applicant. While the Ministry and its offices would be enabled to provide such approvals through appropriate electronic means with the development of the requisite technical environment to receive and validate electronic documents through appropriate means.

Suitable mechanisms are proposed to be evolved to progressively facilitate all transactions from the respective offices of the Ministry with its stakeholders interactively in the electronic mode in respect of matters related to obtaining additional information, clarifications and re-submissions, in addition to the filing of statutory documents.

Implementation of the Programme

Website/Portal and Electronic Registry:

The Government has created a website; www.mca.gov.in and set up a portal accessible through the internet to enable the electronic filing of documents under the scheme. A Data Centre has been set up in Delhi to serve as a Secure Electronic Registry for the storage and retrieval of all the records. A Disaster Recovery Centre has also been set up in Chennai to provide for a back-up of the Electronic Registry to which recourse can be taken in the event of any technology break-down, man-made or natural disaster incapacitating the Data Centre. The operations can be revived within 12 hours in the event of services getting disrupted from the Data Centre. As the sovereign data is managed by an external third party, the project envisages the setting up of a Government Secure Repository (GSR) to which the data would be archived periodically.

The Central Government shall maintain all the records filed electronically in a secure electronic registry to ensure that these are available to the public as well as to the Central Government offices as and when required. The periodicity of maintenance of these records is governed by the rules framed under the Companies Act, 1956. Documents maintained in the electronic registry will be available for public access and shall be weeded out by the retention period prescribed under the rules.

Director Identification Number:

The concept of Director Identification Number (DIN) has been introduced as part of the e-Governance initiative. The need for the introduction of a unique identifier for Directors arose from (*i*) creating a comprehensive and authentic database on the Directors, and the phenomenon of companies that raise funds from the public and subsequently vanish, with their directors becoming untraceable. sections 266A to 266G of Companies (Amendment) Act, 2006, provide for a Director Identification Number (DIN). As part of this scheme, the DIN is in the form of a unique identifier for an existing or a future intending director, containing personal information about such director. This would not only help in fixing the identity of the person but also co-relate his participation in other companies, past or present. A process for allotment of DIN has been put in place duly supported by the provisions contained in the Companies Act, 1956 and the rules made thereunder. It is highlighted that the DIN is a one-time process and, once obtained, the individual will use this in all transactions. Suitable provisions have been made for updating any change in the particulars of a Director in the event of such change occurring after allotment of the DIN in the first stage.

The facility for allotment of DIN has been established even before the introduction of the related provisions in the Companies Act, 1956. The process of system-generated provisional DIN was introduced to enable the companies to transact their businesses where a reference to the DIN was built into the software as necessary. Several persons have generated provisional DINs and used such provisional DINs in their filings. The transactions made by the companies using such provisional DINs during the above transition period shall not be invalid on the ground that the provisional DIN holder had not submitted a formal application for the same. However, after the deadline for obtaining a DIN is reached, the system will allow only the regular DIN to be quoted in filings made thereafter.

e-Forms:

Before the implementation of the e-Governance programme, all transactions, including statutory filings by companies, were conducted in manual mode using the prescribed forms which supported submissions in physical paper form. These Forms have been re-engineered and converted into electronic Forms (e-Forms) to make the same compatible with the e-Governance processes. The e-Forms have already been notified for electronic use. The process of re-engineering and revision of e-Forms is dynamic and may call for changes from time to time depending on the information requirements and technology changes. As such, these e-Forms would continue to be revised as per the felt needs from time to time to optimize the processes under the e-Governance system.

The e-Forms have been designed with in-built features to facilitate stakeholders. Requirements for repetitive data entry have been significantly reduced. Where such data is needed to be repeated in some of the forms, a facility known as "pre-fill" has been provided to the user whereby the data in the required fields is captured from the database available in the electronic registry in an automated manner.

The process of the electronic filing also incorporates the facility of "pre-scrutiny" of the e-Form. This is a completely electronic process where the system verifies if the form is complete in all respects. This is, however, limited to such checks as can be performed by the computerized system.

e-Filing:

It has been decided to mandate electronic filing by the companies from the appointed date to be notified separately. Making the filings in electronic mode would also need the use of methods that ensure the security and authenticity of the filings. It would involve a process according to which the user will be required to—

register himself;
apply for a Director Identification Number (in the case of a Director);
obtain a Digital Signature.

Authentication of Documents with Digital Signatures:

Security and authenticity of filings in electronic mode shall be provided through the use of Digital Signatures by the persons, specified under the Act and Rules made thereunder, to file the documents on behalf of the company. The provisions for use of Digital Signatures have already been made under the Information Technology Act, 2000 and the rules notified by the Central Government on this behalf *vide* Notification GSR 735(E), dated 29-10-2004. As such, all filings made from 16-9-2006 shall be required to be made with the use of Digital Signatures as provided for under various provisions of the Income-tax Act.

Electronic address:

The companies must acquire and communicate an electronic address to the Central Government at which any communications may be sent in the electronic mode. Accordingly, the companies shall be required to interact through the MCA Portal OR use valid e-mail IDs (for themselves or their authorized representatives) to enable the offices of the Central Government to interact with them. This would be necessary for interactions related to the provision of clarifications, additional/supplementary information about a transaction, re-submission of transactions, that were called for, and verification of the status of the progress of transactions.

Attachments:

The filing of various documents including annual returns and balance sheets envisages the attachment of certain documents. Paper source documents will generally need to be scanned/digitized to obtain electronic documents that could be submitted as attachments to e-Forms. Such attachments will need to be in Portable Document Format (PDF).

Where companies maintain and submit their Financial statements as part of Annual Returns and the Balance Sheets (e-Form-20B & Form-23AC) in electronic formats (such as Microsoft(TM) Word or Excel), the same will need to be converted into PDF, thereby obviating the need for scanning these attachments to the extent feasible. For those, who do not have in-house facilities or are first-time users of the system, the MCA Portal and the Facilitation Centres would be available to facilitate the required conversion into PDF. In addition, these facilities would also be available at the Certified Filing Centres (CFCs) for payment of user charges.

There may be some attachments which are much bulkier in size (more than 2.5 MB) where uploading the documents may be time-consuming (for instance, in the case of a list of shareholders of companies with a large base of shareholders). In such cases, the facility for acceptance of these documents in soft-copy in computer-readable media would also be supported.

Physical Submission of Paper:

Notwithstanding the mandating of e-Filing, companies would be required to submit physical copies of the documents requiring the use of non-judicial stamp papers till such time the Central Government introduces a process of electronic generation of stamp papers to facilitate these transactions in complete electronic mode. The documents on stamp papers will be required to be scanned and submitted as attachments to the e- Forms during this period of transition. Physical copies of these documents (on stamp papers) would need to be submitted to the Registrars of Companies in physical form. Such copies may also be sent by companies by post/courier. In cases of physical submission, appropriate transaction reference details such as the Service Request Number (SRN) would also be required to be mentioned on the physical paper documents.

Scanning and Digitization of Company Records:

The Central Government has scanned and digitized the permanent documents of companies and the Annual Return and Balance Sheets for two years and thus created an electronic repository of part of the legacy data. All event-based filings by the companies immediately preceding the launch of the programme have also been captured in the electronic repository. It is expected that the data in the electronic Registry would get enriched substantially over some time as the electronic filings of Companies will seamlessly add to the legacy records.

Inspection of Public Documents:

The inspection of public documents was earlier carried out by inspection of physical files containing company documents available in the concerned RoC offices. The documents, in so far as these are available in digitized form, shall henceforth be available for public inspection through electronic means using the Internet. However, after the implementation of the e-Governance programme, the documents have been filed only in electronic form and these are available only in electronic form. The users will have the option of looking at an index of documents available in electronic format. The documents can be accessed electronically upon payment of the statutory fees for a limited duration from the time of accessing the first document of the given company. In case of the documents are not available in the electronic repository, the same can be viewed in person from the concerned RoC office in paper form and no fresh payment of the fee would be required if the proof of payment for electronic viewing is produced at the RoC office.

Requests for Certified Copies:

Requests for certified copies would also be facilitated through electronic means with the implementation of the programme. This functionality is built as an extension of the Inspection of Public Documents, where the user can mark the specified pages and the number of copies that are required as certified copies. In case of documents available in the electronic registry, a person can request for certified copies of the selected documents online (on payment of prescribed fees). The requestor would also be required to submit the Non-Judicial Stamp Papers of the prescribed value and Court Fee, as applicable in various States. The certified copies of the documents will be sent in physical form to the requester by post/courier under the manual signatures and seal of the competent authority. However, in respect of documents not available in the electronic registry, the option of requesting certified copies in the manual form will still be available. Prescribed fees will be applicable.

Data Verification & Cleaning

Before implementation of the e-Governance programme described in this scheme, the company records were filed and received in the manual mode in the offices of Registrars and as per the rules and practices of maintenance of manual records, these documents formed part of the Document files of respective companies. As part of the operations, the limited amount of data about companies was maintained in computerized systems using the system of manual data entry. It was observed on test checks that there were inaccuracies in the Data of Companies so entered and maintained.

The existing data has been migrated to the new e-Governance system. As a result, the migrated database is likely to carry over these inaccuracies in the electronic repository and, despite best efforts, it may not be possible to clean the same. To ensure an authentic database in respect of all the companies, Central Government may call upon the companies to verify the existing data which can be viewed online without any charge.

A facility has been provided whereby the companies can access their Master Company Data. In case it is found that the Company Data is incorrect in respect of certain fields, the company would be required to enter the correct data against the appropriate field, enclose a copy of the evidence supporting such correction and send the same by post to the concerned Registrar of Companies in an envelope superscribed 'Master Company Data Correction'. Upon receipt of the request, the requisite changes would be incorporated after verification of the supporting evidence.

The facility of correction of Company Data has been made available without any charge only for a limited period (up to 31-12-2006). Accordingly, all the companies would be requested through public notices (both through the print media and the portal) to view their Company Master Data and take appropriate steps for correcting the same.

A similar facility has also been made available in respect of the 'Register of Charges' for the companies.

Where, for any reason, a company encounters difficulty in using the new e- Governance programme, it may contact the respective Registrar of Companies or the staff in the Facilitation Centres who will facilitate electronic filing.

Investor Complaints and Grievance Handling:

Suitable forms have been devised for investors to make complaints and for a complainant to seek redressal of his grievances in the electronic mode using the e-Governance programme. The idea behind instituting the electronic submission of complaints is to ensure that complete details of the complaint are obtained so that the facilitation of redressal can be done effectively. It also provides a facility to consolidate the type of complaints that are received against any company, so that the company can effectively analyze the causes and take remedial action. The persistent complaints and serious nature of complaints also provide the Government with early indicators of problems in companies so that reasonable steps can be taken as provided by the Law, to protect the interest of the investors/ depositors/stakeholders.

The communication to the companies as well as the complainants would be sent in paper mode during the initial period. This would gradually be phased out and replaced with electronic interaction response.

Facilitates to provide the management information on complaints to the company Directors/Authorized Representatives would be implemented as part of the scheme in due course of time.

Payment of Statutory Fees:

The filings by the companies entail payment of statutory fees, wherever prescribed. Multiple options are available for remittance of statutory fees under which the users may opt for an 'off-line' mode of payment or 'on-line' mode of payment. In the case of the offline mode of payment, the system calculates the applicable fees and generates a pre-filled challan, which the user would be required to present before one of the Authorized Bank Branches for making payment. The list of Authorized Bank Branches has been made available on the portal of the Ministry and updated from time to time. In case the user opts for an online mode of payment, he has been given the option to use Credit Card (Master Card or VISA) or Internet Banking. The Internet Banking facility is in the process of being made available under MCA21 and is expected to be operational soon. In the case of online payment, the system generates a receipt of the fee amount paid by the user.

The use of online payment modes allows the facility of instant realisation of payment of statutory fees and enables faster delivery of services. As against this, in the off-line mode of payment, it may take a lead time of about 3-4 days for the Banks to intimate about the realization of payment to the system. The service request gets activated only after confirmation of payment is received from the Bank.

Keeping in view the possibility of duplicate payments in respect of the same services under the online payment system, or payments made more than those prescribed, a refund process is proposed to be introduced whereby the refunds could be allowed in cases of duplicate/excess payments in genuine cases. However, the cases in which such requests for refunds would be entertained would be specifically indicated in the refund process.

Availability of Services and Sustainability:

The Government has put in place processes for taking the documents electronically filed by the companies on record, completing the processing thereof and maintaining the records in the Electronic Registry for access to the public and the Central Government as per requirement.

To ensure the sustainable performance of the e-Governance solution, the Government has established a six-year operating period with the selected Operator. Beyond this period, Ministry would evolve a suitable structure to seamlessly operate the same. Such a structure could include the setting up of a Special Purpose Vehicle (SPV) and could entail the introduction of user charges for sustaining the operations of such an entity.

The services under the e-Governance project shall be available to the stakeholders on a round-the-clock basis throughout the week basis thereby enabling the introduction of the concept of anywhere, anytime securely filing in the electronic mode for all transactions with and by the Ministry of Company Affairs. But for exigencies beyond reasonable control, the Operator has been made responsible under the contract for maintaining reliable availability of the system to support this concept.

Facilitation Centres:

As for the facilitation, the Government has planned to set up Facilitation Centres at 53 locations throughout the country as part of the project out of which Facilitation Centres at 39 locations have already been set up. All services from these Centres are available free of charge. These Centres, managed and operated by the Operator, would remain operational for three years, by which time it is expected that the stakeholders would have switched over to e-filing from their virtual offices. The Ministry has also introduced a scheme of Certified Filing Centres (CFCs) to provide a much wider outreach of the facilitation services. These CFCs will be managed and operated by the professionals (Chartered Accountants, Company Secretaries, Cost & Works Accountants and the body corporates managed by these professionals) and the services would be provided on a user-charge basis. The Government may review, modify or introduce newer schemes from time to time to facilitate e-filings by companies.

The Government would strongly encourage the stakeholders to optimally use the facilities available under the e-governance programme from the comfort of their offices or homes and transact all business online from their virtual offices. However, in case the company representatives/professionals/stakeholders face any difficulties in using the system and the facilities from their virtual offices, for whatsoever reasons, adequate support and help would be available at the facilitation centres. However, for the filing of documents, the stakeholders would be required to bring their filings (e-forms and attachments duly authenticated with Digital Signatures) in soft copies at these centres in computer-readable media such as floppies or CDs or USB tokens.

Help Desk:

In a large-scale Transition involving migration from a traditional paper-based system to an e-Governance system, extensive facilitation and help would be needed by the stakeholders. With this in mind, a help system has been provided at three levels:

- through a central call centre with phone numbers published on the MCA portal;
- e-mail facility that can be accessed through the portal;
- at the various Front Offices/Facilitation Centres.

Performance Factors:

It is expected that the responses provided would be resulting from the combined performance levels of the system responses (including system availability), the performance of the facilitation centres, the timelines of payment acknowledgements from Banks and the processing time required by the offices of MCA. The Government will progressively evolve monitorable and measurable levels of performance at each level so that the overall efficiencies in service delivery standards could be measured against service benchmarks comparable with those obtained in the developed economies of the world.

Presently, these service levels are defined in the Citizen Charter. It is expected that there would be an improvement over the timelines mentioned Citizen Charter as the e-Governance programme progresses dynamically. The MCA would publish these service benchmarks after complete stabilization of the system operations.

Process Changes:

The e-Governance programme shall be developed around a set of detailed processes, basically designed to be easily adaptive to scalability while accommodating changes to technology or other solution components.

The processes could also be impacted due to changes in law and also based on the evolution that is expected to occur with time.

It may also be provided that where a filing does not require any immediate processing or approval, it may be taken on record through the 'Straight Through Process (STP) to be implemented through amendment of the relevant regulation.

Central Government may also introduce the process of electronic generation of stamp papers in due course of time after the required authorizations have been received from the states, to eliminate the process of submission of physical documents.

The process innovations would entail changes and MCA will provide enough lead time including public announcements and information through the MCA portal for the benefit of users of this system.

3.7 MCA 21(MINISTRY OF CORPORATE AFFAIRS)

MCA regulates corporate affairs in India through the Companies Act, 1956, 2013 and other allied Acts, Bills and Rules. MCA also protects investors and offers many important services to stakeholders. This site is your gateway to all services, guidance, and other corporate affairs-related information.

The Ministry is also responsible for administering the Competition Act, 2002 to prevent practices having adverse effects on competition, promote and sustain competition in markets, and protect the interests of consumers through the commission set up under the Act.

The Ministry also has the responsibility of carrying out the functions of the Central Government relating to the administration of the Partnership Act, 1932, the Companies (Donations to National Funds) Act, 1951 and the Societies Registration Act, 1980.

- **Objective**

The MCA21 application is designed to fully automate all processes related to the proactive enforcement and compliance of the legal requirements under the Companies Act, 1956, New Companies Act, 2013 and Limited Liability Partnership Act, 2008. This will help the business community to meet its statutory obligations.

3.7.1 BENEFITS(FEATURES)

- Enables the business community to register a company and file statutory documents quickly and easily.
- Provides easy access to public documents
- Helps faster and more effective resolution of public grievances.

- Helps registration and verification of charges easily.
- Ensures proactive and effective compliance with relevant laws and corporate governance
- Enables the MCA employees to deliver best-of-breed services.

3.7.2 SERVICES OFFERED

Obtain Digital Signature Certificate - The Information Technology Act, 2000 has provisions for use of Digital Signatures on the documents submitted in the electronic form to ensure the security and authenticity of the documents filed electronically.

This is a secure and authentic way to submit a document electronically. As such, all filings done by the companies/ LLPs under the MCA21 e-Governance programme are required to be filed using Digital Signatures by the person authorized to sign the documents.

Apply for Director Identification Number (DIN) - The concept of a Director Identification Number (DIN) has been introduced with the insertion of Sections 266A to 266G of the Companies (Amendment) Act, 2006. As such, all the existing and intending Directors have to obtain DIN within the prescribed time frame as notified.

View master Details of any Company/LLP Registered with the Registrar of Companies - A facility has been made available to the general public to view master details of any company/LLP registered with the Registrar of Companies. This facility may be availed by clicking "View Company Master Data".

A similar facility has also been made available in respect of the 'Register of Charges' for the companies/LLPs by clicking on the 'View Index of Charges' and for viewing the details of the signatories of any company/LLP by clicking on 'View Signatory Details.

e-Filing for Limited Liability Partnership (LLP) - To carry out e-Filing on LLP, a facility to download the form and fill it in an offline mode is available. Every form has the facility to pre-fill the data available in the LLP system. Once the e-form is filled, it has to be validated using the Pre-scrutiny button. The relevant digital signatures have to be affixed and the form saved. A user has to be connected to the internet to carry out the pre-fill and pre-scrutiny

- LLP Services for Business User
- Registration of a new Company
- Raise complaints or concerns concerning MCA services
- Document Related Services
- Fee and Payment Services
- Investor Services

CHAPTER FOUR

MEMORANDUM OF ASSOCIATION AND ARTICLES OF ASSOCIATION

Memorandum of Association - Nature and Content of Memorandum - Alteration of Memorandum - Doctrine of Ultra Vires - Articles of Association - Purpose and Content of Articles -Alteration of Articles - Doctrine of Constructive Notice and Indoor Management.

4.1 A MEMORANDUM OF ASSOCIATION (MOA)

A Memorandum of Association is one of the documents which have to be filed with the Registrar of Companies at the time of incorporation of a company. It is a document which sets out the constitution of the company and is really the foundation on which the structure of the company is based. It contains the fundamental conditions upon which alone the company is allowed to be incorporated. A company may pursue only such objects and exercise only A company cannot depart from the provisions constrained in its memorandum, however, great the necessity maybe if it does, it would be ultra vires the company and therefore wholly void. It defines its relationship with the outside world and the relation with the outside world and the scope of its activities. The purpose of the memorandum is to enable shareholders, creditors and those who deal with the company to know what is the permitted range of the activities of the enterprise.

Meaning

- A Memorandum of Association (MOA) is a legal document prepared in the formation and registration process of a limited liability company to define its relationship with shareholders. The MOA is accessible to the public and describes the company's name, physical address of registered office, names of shareholders and the distribution of shares.
- According to **Section 2(56)** of the Companies Act 2013, the "Memorandum" refers to the memorandum of the company as drawn up initially during the formation of the company or as changed periodically to carry out any action as per any other law of the Act.
- The MOA and the Articles of Association serve as the constitution of the company. The MOA is not applied in the U.S. but is a legal requirement for limited liability companies in European countries including the United Kingdom, France and Netherlands, as well as some Commonwealth nations.

In other Words

A Memorandum of Association (MoA) represents the charter of the company. It is a legal document prepared during the formation and registration process of a company to define its relationship with shareholders and it specifies the objectives for which the company has been formed. The company can undertake only those activities that are mentioned in the Memorandum of Association. As such, the MoA lays down the boundary beyond which the actions of the company cannot go.

- Memorandum of Association helps the shareholders, creditors and any other person dealing with the company to know the basic rights and powers of the company. Also, the contents of the MoA help prospective shareholders in taking the right decision while thinking of investing in the company.
- MoA must be signed by at least 2 subscribers in case of a private limited company, and 7 members in case of a public limited company.

The memorandum of association of a company is an important corporate document in India. It is often simply referred to as the memorandum. In India, it has to be filed with the Registrar of Companies during the process of incorporating a company.

It is the document that regulates the company's external affairs and complements the articles of association which cover the company's internal constitution. It contains the fundamental conditions under which the company is allowed to operate. Until recently it had to include the "objects clause" which let the shareholders, creditors and those dealing with the company know what is its permitted range of operation, although this was usually drafted very broadly. It also shows the company's Authorized capital. Read some important aspects of same.

4.1.1 OBJECT OF REGISTERING A MEMORANDUM OF ASSOCIATION OR MOA

- The MOA of a company contains the object for which the company is formed. It identifies the scope of its operations and determines the boundaries it cannot cross.
- It is a public document according to Section 399 of the Companies Act, 2013. Hence, any person who enters into a contract with the company is expected to know the MOA.
- It contains details about the powers and rights of the company.

4.1.2 FORMAT OF MEMORANDUM OF ASSOCIATION (MOA)

According to Section 4 of the Companies Act, 2013, companies must draw the MOA in the form given in Tables A-E in Schedule I of the Act. Here are the details of the forms:

- **Table A:** Form for the memorandum of association of a company limited by shares.
- **Table B:** Form for the memorandum of association of a company limited by guarantee and not having a share capital.
- **Table C:** Form for the memorandum of association of a company limited by guarantee and having a share capital.
- **Table D:** Form for the memorandum of association of an unlimited company.
- **Table E:** Form for the memorandum of association of an unlimited company and having a share capital.

4.1.3 WHAT ARE THE PRESCRIBED FORMS OF MOA?

Table A: A company limited by shares

Table B: A company limited by guarantee and not having a share capital

Table C: A company limited by guarantee and having a share capital

Table D: An unlimited company

Table E: An unlimited company having a share capital

4.1.4 CONTENT OF THE MOA

According to section 13, the memorandum of association of every company must contain the following clauses.

What are the different parts of the Memorandum of Association (MOA)?

A Memorandum of Association (MOA) is an important document which outlines the company laws under which a company will work and function. It has several clauses which define some pertinent aspects under the provision of The Companies Act, 2013 which are as follows:-

1. Name Clause
2. Situation/ Registered State Clause
3. Object clause
4. Liability clause
5. Capital Clause
6. Subscriber Clause

Now lets us discuss them in detail.

1. The name of the company with 'limited ' as the last word of the name in the case of a public limited company and with 'private limited ' as the last word in the case of a private limited company.
2. The state in which the registered office of the company is to be situated.
3. the objects of the company to be classified as

   i. the main objects of the company to be pursued by the company on its incorporation and objects incidental to the attainments of the main objects, &
   ii. Other objects not included above, limited if the company is limited by; shares or by guarantee.

4. The liability of members is limited if the company is limited by shares or by guarantee.
5. In the case of a company having a share capital, the amount of share capital with which the company proposes to be registered and its division into shares of a fixed amount. An unlimited company need not include items 4 and 5 in its memorandum a brief discussion of the various clauses is as follows:

4.1.5 INFORMATION IS MANDATORY IN AN MOA

Name Clause:

A company may be registered with any name it likes. But no company shall be and in particular which is identical or which too nearly resembles the name of an existing company. Every public company must write the word 'limited' after its name and every private limited' after its name. A company cannot adopt a name which violates the provisions of the Emblems and Names [Prevention of Improper Use] Act 1950. every company is required to publish its name outside its registered office, and outside every place where it carries on business, to have its name engraved on a seal and to have its name on all business letters, bill heads, notices and other official publications of the company [Section 147].

- For a public limited company, the name of the company must have the word 'Limited' as the last word
- For the private limited company, the name of the company must have the words 'Private Limited' as the last words.
- This does not apply to companies formed under Section 8 of the Act who must include one of the following words, as applicable:
- Foundation
- Forum

- Association
- Federation
- Chambers
- Confederation
- Council
- Electoral Trust, etc.

Registered Office Clause:

It must specify the State in which the registered office of the company will be situated. This clause states the name of the State where the registered office of the company is to be situated. The registered office clause is important for two reasons. Firstly, it ascertains the domicile and nationality of a company. This domicile clings to it throughout its existence. Secondly, it is the place where various registers relating to the company must be kept and to which all communications and notices must be sent.

Object Clause:

It must specify the objects for which the company is being incorporated. Further, if a company changes its activities which are not reflected in its name, then it can change its name within six months of changing its activities. The company must comply with all name-change provisions.

The object clause is the most important in the memorandum of association of a company. It is not merely a record of what is contemplated by the subscribers, but it serves a two-fold purpose.

a. It gives an idea to the prospective shareholders of the purposes for which their money will be utilized.
b. It enables the persons dealing with the company to ascertain its powers in the case of companies which were in existence immediately before the commencement of the companies [Amendment Act 1965, the objects clause has simply to state the objects of the company to be registered after the amendment, the objects clause must state the objects of the company. But in the case of a company to be registered after the amendment, the objects clause must state separately.

i) Main Objects:

This sub-clause has to state the main objects to be pursued by the company on its incorporation and objects incidental or ancillary to the attainment of the main objects.

ii) Other Objects

This sub-clause shall state other objects which are not included in the above clause.

Liability Clause:

- It should specify the liability of the members of the company, whether limited or unlimited. Also,
- **For a company limited by shares** – it should specify if the liability of its members is limited to any unpaid amount on the shares that they hold.
- **For a company limited by guarantee** – it should specify the amount undertaken by each member to contribute to:
    - The assets of the company when it winds up. This is provided that he is a member of the company when it winds up or the winding up happens within one year of him ceasing to be a member. In the latter case, the debts and liabilities considered would be those contracted before he ceases to be a member.
    - The costs, charges, and expenses of winding up and the adjustment of the rights of the contributors among themselves.

Capital Clause:

This is valid only for companies having a share capital. These companies must specify the amount of Authorized capital divided into shares of fixed amounts. Further, it must state the names of each member and the number of shares against their names.

The memorandum of a company limited by shares must state the authorized or nominal share capital, the different kinds of shares, and the nominal value of each share. the chief point to consider regarding this clause is what funds are necessary to set the business going or, if it is proposed by an existing concern, what sum is needed to pay its price and what, in addition, is wanted to keep the business going. It is generally advisable to have a reasonable amount of more capital and have some shares in reserve as unissued so that further capital may be raised as and when required.

Association Clause:

The MOA must specify the desire of the subscriber to form a company. This is the last clause.

- **For One-Person-Company**
- The MOA must specify the name of the person who becomes a member of the company in the event of the death of the subscriber.
- Keep in mind the following aspects before submitting the MOA:
- Print the MOA
- Divide it into paragraphs
- Number the pages in sequence
- Ensure that at least seven people sign it (2 in the case of a private limited company and one in the case of a One Person company).
- Have at least one witness to attest the signatures

Enter particulars about the signatories and witnesses like address, description, occupation,

4.1.6 WHY IS A MEMORANDUM OF ASSOCIATION NECESSARY FOR A COMPANY?

A memorandum of association allows people like the shareholders, creditors, investors and other members of a company to know the purpose for which a company has been formed. It allows them to know the range of activities that the company is permitted to be involved in and authorizes them to learn about the company's objectives.

The memorandum of association also curbs the company's flexibility by preventing it from getting involved in any kind of activities other than the ones mentioned in the memorandum while the company is in its initial stages of formation.

Some definitions and purposes of the Memorandum of Association as observed by judges such as **Lord Cairns**, **Lord Macmillan**, **Lord Selborne** and **Charles Worth** in historical cases can be accessed here.

4.1.7 WHAT'S THE IMPORTANCE OF THE MEMORANDUM OF ASSOCIATION?

Determines the Area of Operation:

It provides a list of activities that an organization can undertake. Apart from this list, any other operation will be void.

Determines the Relationship of the Company with Outsiders:

The sole purpose of this document is to disperse the necessary information to the shareholders, creditors and other stakeholders. It showcases the range of enterprise and its powers of it.

Fixed Charter of the Company:

The memorandum of association is considered a fixed charter for the company (as per section 16 of the Companies Act).

Basis of Incorporation:

You need to file the memorandum of association with the registrar of the companies to get it incorporated. For this, it should be signed by at least 7 persons in the case of a public company and 2 persons in the case of a private company.

4.1.8 WHAT'S THE USE OF THE MEMORANDUM OF ASSOCIATION?

The Memorandum of Association (MoA) helps establish the extent and scope of the business activities that a particular company can carry out. The company can perform business activities that they have specified in the Memorandum of Association (MoA). If you wish to expand your business activities into other areas of the market, you will have to make changes to the memorandum accordingly.

A Memorandum of Association (MOA) is a legal document applicable to limited liability companies. Limited Liability Companies include Private Limited Company (Pvt Ltd) and Limited Liability Partnership (LLP). MOA is used to define the company's relationship with the shareholders. The MOA is a document of public record i.e. anyone who wishes to see a company's MoA can do so under the Right to Information (RTI) Act. MoA also describes the company's name, the physical address of the registered office, the names of shareholders and the distribution of shares. Sometimes, MoA also contains exemptions and tweaks for a particular company. For eg., Private Limited Companies have a lot of exemptions as compared to other companies. Read Exemptions Private Limited Company.

The MOA and the Articles of Association (AOA) put together, serve as the constitution of the company. The MOA is not applied in the U.S. but is a legal requirement for limited liability companies in European countries including the United Kingdom, France, and the Netherlands, as well as some Commonwealth nations.

SAMPLE

Sample of Memorandum of a Company Limited by Shares

XYZ Private Limited, a company, situated in Punjab, is engaged in the business of manufacturing security devices. It wants to register with the Registrar of Companies. For registration, the company has to first subscribe to a memorandum.

The Memorandum of Association of XYZ Private Limited will look like this:

(Since XYZ Private Limited is a company limited by shares, the form given in Table A will apply to it.)

The Companies Act, 2013

Company Limited by Shares

Memorandum of Association

Of

XYZ Private Limited

1. The name of the company is XYZ Private Limited. *(Name Clause)*
2. The registered office of the company will be situated in the state of Punjab. *(Registered Office Clause)*

3. The object for which the company is established is *(Object Clause):*

(a) The objects to be pursued by the company on its incorporation are:

I. To carry on the business of manufacturing, converting, altering, designing, and producing security systems.
II. To trade, buy, sell or act as agents to import or export all security-related devices.
III. To carry on the business and act as buyers, sellers, traders, agents and dealers for obtaining the above objects.

(*b*) Matters which are necessary for the furtherance of the objects specified in clause 3A are:

1. To manufacture and deal in packaging materials, boxes, grading, branding, weighting, and marketing for all kinds of security devices and other electronic components associated with them.

2. To draw, make, accept, endorse, discount, execute, issue, negotiate, assign and otherwise deal with cheques, drafts, bills of exchange, promissory notes, hundies, debentures, bonds, bills of lading, railway receipts, warrants and all other negotiable or transferable instruments.
3. To amalgamate with any other company or companies.
4. To acquire or merge with any other company.
5. To start a joint venture with any other company.
6. To distribute any of the property of the Company amongst the members in specie or kind subject to the provisions of the Companies Act in the event of winding up.
7. To apply for, tender, purchase, or otherwise acquire any contracts, subcontracts licences and concessions for or about the objects or business herein mentioned or any of them, and to undertake, execute, carry out, dispose of or otherwise turn to account the same.

- The liability of the member(s) is limited and this liability is limited to the amount unpaid, if any, on the shares held by them. *(Liability Clause)*

- The share capital of the company is 70,00,000 rupees, divided into 2000 shares of 3500 rupees each. *(Capital Clause)*
- We, the several persons, whose names and addresses are subscribed, are desirous of being formed into a company in pursuance of this memorandum of association, and we respectively agree to take the number of shares in the capital of the company set against our respective names:

4.1.10 WHO CAN SUBSCRIBE?

Rule 13 of the Companies (Incorporation) Rules, 2014 describes the provisions of subscribing to the memorandum. There are specific kinds of persons (natural or artificial) who can subscribe to the memorandum. These are:

1. *Individuals* – An individual or a group of individuals can subscribe to the memorandum.
2. *Foreign citizens and Non-Resident Indians* – Rule 13(5) of the Companies (Incorporation) Rules, states that for a foreign citizen to subscribe to a company in India, his signature, address and proof of identity will need to be notarized.

The foreign national must have visited India and should have a Business Visa.

For a Non-Resident Indian, the photograph, address and identity proof should be attested at the Embassy with a certified copy of a passport. There is no requirement for Business Visa.

1. *Minor* – A minor can only be a subscriber through his guardian.
2. *Company incorporated under the Companies Act* – The company can be a subscriber to the memorandum. The Director, officer or employee of the company or any other person authorized by the board of resolution.
3. *Company incorporated outside India* – Foreign Company is defined in Section 2(42) of the act, which states that a foreign company is a company incorporated outside India. A company registered outside India can also subscribe to the memorandum by fulfilling the additional formalities.
4. *Society registered under the Societies Registration Act, 1860.*
5. *Limited Liability Partnership* – A partner of a limited liability partnership can sign the memorandum with the agreement of all the other partners.
6. *Body corporate incorporated* under an Act of Parliament or State Legislature can also be a subscriber to the memorandum.

Subscription to Memorandum of Association

Every subscriber should sign the memorandum in presence of at least one witness. The following particulars of the witness should also be mentioned.

1. Name of the witness
2. Address
3. Description
4. Occupation

If the signature is in any other language then, then an affidavit is required that declares that the signature is the actual signature of the person.

According to Circular No. 8/15/8, dated 1-9-1958. The subscriber can also authorize another person to affix the signature by granting a power of attorney to the person. Department Circular No. 1/95, dated 16th February 1995 states that only one power of attorney is required.

The person who is granted the power of attorney may be known as an agent.

He should also state the following particulars in the memorandum:

1. Name of the agent
2. Address
3. Description
4. Occupation

4.1.11 PARTICULARS TO BE MENTIONED IN MEMORANDUM OF ASSOCIATION

Rule 16 of the Companies (Incorporation) Rules, 2014 details the particulars that are to be mentioned in the memorandum.

Every Subscriber's following details should be mentioned.

1. Name (includes last name and family name), a photograph should be affixed and scanned with the memorandum.
2. Father's Name and Mother's Name
3. Nationality
4. Date of Birth
5. Place of Birth
6. Qualifications
7. Occupation
8. Permanent Account Number
9. Permanent and Current Address
10. Contact Number
11. Fax Number (Optional)
12. 2 Identity Proofs in which Permanent Account Number is mandatory.
13. Residential Proof (not older than 2 months)
14. Proof of nationality, if the subscriber is a foreign national
15. If the subscriber is a current director or promoter, then his designation along with his Name and Company Identity Number

If a body corporate is subscribing to the memorandum then the following particulars should be mentioned.

1. Corporate identity number of the company or registration number of the body corporate.
2. Global location number, which is used to identify the location of the legal entity. (Optional)
3. The name of the body corporate.
4. The registered address of the business.
5. Email address.

In case the body corporate is a company, then a certified copy of the Board resolution authorizes the subscription to the memorandum. The particulars required in this case are,

1. Number of shares to be subscribed by a body corporate.
2. Name, designation and address of the authorized person.

In case the body corporate is a limited liability partnership. The particulars required are,

1. A certified copy of the resolution.
2. The number of shares that the firm is subscribing to.
3. The name of the authorized partner.

In case the body corporate is registered outside the country. The particulars required are,

1. The copy of the certificate of incorporation.
2. The address of the registered office.

4.1.12 PRINTING AND SIGNING OF MEMORANDUM OF ASSOCIATION

Section 7(1)(a) states that the memorandum should be duly signed by all the subscribers and should be in a manner prescribed by the Act.

Rule 13 of the Company (Incorporation) Rules, 2014 describes how the memorandum should be signed.

The Memorandum of Association should be signed by each subscriber to the memorandum. The subscriber shall mention his name, address, occupation and the number of shares he is subscribing to. The documents should be signed in the presence of at least one witness. The witness would also mention his name, address, and occupation. By signing the memorandum, the witness states that "I witness to subscriber/subscriber(s)who has/have subscribed and signed in my presence (date and place to be given); further I have verified his or their Identity Details (ID) for their identification and satisfied myself of his/her/their identification particulars as filled in."

If the person subscribing to the document is illiterate, he can either authorize an agent to sign the document through Power of Attorney or he can put his thumb impression on the column for signatures. The person's name, address, occupation and the number of shares he is subscribing to should be written by a person who has been allowed to write for him. The person who is writing for the illiterate person should read and explain the contents of the document to an illiterate person.

Where the person subscribing to the memorandum is an artificial person i. e. a body corporate the memorandum shall be signed by the employee, officer or any person authorized by the Board of Resolution.

Where the person subscribing to the memorandum is a foreign national who does not reside in India but a country,

- in any part of the Commonwealth, his signatures and address on the memorandum and proof of identity shall be notarized by a Notary (Public) in that part of the Commonwealth.
- in a country which is a signatory to the Hague Apostille Convention, 1961, his signature and proof of identity and address on the memorandum shall be notarized before the Notary (Public) of the country of his origin and be duly approved by the said Hague Convention.
- in a country outside the Commonwealth and which is not a party to the Hague Apostille Convention, 1961, his signatures and address on the memorandum and proof of identity, shall be notarized before the Notary (Public) of such country and the certificate of the Notary (Public) shall be authenticated by a Diplomatic or Consular Officer empowered in this behalf under section 3 of the Diplomatic and Consular Officers (Oaths and Fees) Act, 1948 (40 of 1948).

Section 3 of the Diplomatic and Consular Officers states that every Diplomat or any officer in a foreign country can perform the functions of a notary public.

1. Where there is no Diplomatic or Consular officer by any of the officials mentioned in section 6 of the Commissioners of Oaths Act, 1889.
2. If the foreign national visited India and intended to incorporate a company, in such a case the incorporation shall be allowed if, he is having a valid Business Visa.

Section 15 of the Companies Act, 2013 states that the memorandum should be in printed form.

The Ministry of Corporate Affairs has clarified that a document printed in the form of laser printers will be considered valid provided it is legible and fulfils other requirements as well.

The submission of xerox copies is not allowed. The xerox copies can be submitted to the members of the company.

4.1.13 ALTERATION, AMENDMENT & CHANGE IN MEMORANDUM OF ASSOCIATION UNDER COMPANIES ACT, 2013.

The term "alter" or "alteration" is defined in Section 2(3) of the Act, as any additions, omissions or substitutions. A company can alter the memorandum only to the extent permitted by the Act. According to Section 13, the company can alter the clauses in the memorandum by passing a special resolution.

A resolution is a formal decision taken in a meeting. There are two kinds of resolutions, ordinary and special. A special resolution requires at least a $2/3^{rd}$ majority to be effective. The alteration to the clauses also requires the approval of the Central Government in writing.

The alteration of the memorandum can happen for a variety of reasons. The alteration can be made if,

1. Enables the company to carry it's business more effectively;
2. Helps to achieve the objectives;
3. Helps the company to amalgamate with another company;
4. Helps the company dispose of any undertaking.

4.2 ALTERATION OF MEMORANDUM

The provisions of the Act rigidly limit the memorandum of association of a company being its charter, the right of the company to alter its contents. Section 16 of the Act provides that a company shall not alter the conditions contained in its memorandum except in the cases, in the manner and to the extent provided in the Act. Alteration in the Memorandum of Association can be carried out only by a special resolution at the Shareholders' meeting. This is a complicated and lengthy procedure. So Memorandum must be very carefully prepared at the beginning itself.

4.2.1 PROVISIONS RELATING TO ALTERATION OF MEMORANDUM

The following are the provisions related to alteration in the Name Clause, Objects Clause, Liability Clause, Capital Clause and Subscription Clause.

Alteration of Name Clause in Memorandum of Association:

A company may by passing a special resolution alter its name with the approval of the Central Government. If the alteration involves a change of the name to private limited or public limited, the permission of the Central Government is not required.

In case a company has been registered with a name which resembles a name of an existing company, the Central Government may ask it to change its name. In such case ordinary resolution is sufficient.

The intimation of name change should be given to the Registrar who will issue a fresh certificate of incorporation.

Alteration of Situation clause

1. In case the registered office has to be shifted within the same city, town or village, a notice has to be given to the Registrar within thirty days of the change.
2. In case the registered office has to be shifted from one town to another town or one village to another village, a special resolution has to be passed.
3. A company can change its registered office from one State to another State for the following reasons:

a. to carry on business more efficiently and economically;
b. to achieve the important purpose of the company by sophisticated means;
c. to expand its operations in the current location;
d. to control any of the existing objects;
e. to sell whole or part of the business undertaking;
f. to amalgamate with other businesses or people.

In case, the registered office has to be shifted from one State to another State, a special resolution has to be passed and approval from the Company Law Board has to be obtained by the company. The altered memorandum should be filed with the Registrar of the State from which the company is shifting and also with the Registrar of the State to which the company is shifting.

Alteration of Objects Clause in Memorandum of Association:

A company can alter its object clause by passing a special resolution. Alteration of objects clause can be done for the following reasons:

1. to carry on its business more economically and efficiently.
2. to obtain the main business of the company by new and improved means
3. to enlarge or change the local area of its operations.
4. to carry on some business, which may be conveniently or advantageously combined with the existing business.
5. to abandon any of the objects specified in the memorandum.
6. to sell the whole or any part of the undertaking.
7. to amalgamate with any other company.

Alteration of Liability Clause in Memorandum of Association:

The liability clause can be altered only when a public company is converted to a private company.

Alteration of Capital Clause in Memorandum of Association:

A company can alter its capital clause by passing an ordinary resolution in a general meeting. Alteration of capital may relate to:

i. Sub-division of shares

ii. consolidation of shares
iii. conversion of shares into stock and cancellation of unsubscribed capital.

Within thirty days of passing a resolution, the altered Articles and Memorandum have to be submitted to the Registrar.

Alteration of subscription clause in Memorandum of Association:

The company can alter its subscription clause to make the liability of the directors appointed after the alteration unlimited.

4.2.2 What provisions/section governs the alteration/changes of the Memorandum of Association (MOA)?

Section 13 of The Companies Act, 2013 governs the process and conditions for alteration in the Memorandum of Association (MOA). The following clauses can be changed as per this section-

1. Name Clause
2. Situation Clause
3. Object Clause
4. Capital Clause

However, they are also supported by other sections to give effect to respective changes.

Note that the Subscription clause can never be altered after the Company's incorporation.

What are the forms to be filed for alteration/changes of the Memorandum of Association (MOA)?

Different forms are filed to Registrar according to the changed MOA clause and all have to be filled within the time prescribed under the required forms and sections.

What if the company failed to comply with the alteration/change in the Memorandum of Association (MOA) as per law?

As per **section 13** of The Companies Act, 2013 until/unless all provisions and forms/ returns are not filled as per law, the alteration in the Memorandum of Association stands nullified.

Disclaimer: – The above article is prepared to keep in mind various provisions relating to the Memorandum of association (MOA) under the Companies Act, 2013 and the rules made thereunder. The author has tried to cover all the important and basic questions relating to the Memorandum of association (MOA) and its alteration thereunder. Under no circumstance, the author shall not liable for any direct, indirect, special or incidental damage resulting from, arising out of or in connection with the use of the information.

(The Author is a Corporate Consultant and provides a varied array of services including Start-ups mentor, Secretarial, Legal, Trademark, taxation, Audit, GST, Bookkeeping and other ancillary advisory service in Delhi, Chandigarh as well as The National Capital Region (NCR) and

4.3 DOCTRINE OF ULTRA – VIRUS

The term "Ultra" means beyond and "Vires" means powers. The term, therefore, means the doing of an act, which is beyond the legal power, and authority of the company. It is considered an act outside the scope of the object of the company.

4.3.1 DOCTRINE OF ULTRA VIRUS

The Memorandum, being the constitution of the company sets out the principal objectives, powers, scope and its area of operation, both internal and external. A company, therefore, can do anything within the scope of the powers specified in the Memorandum. It has also an implied power to do all such things that are fairly incidental to its main objects. If the company does anything which is beyond the powers specified in the Memorandum it shall be construed as an Ultra Virus act.

4.3.2 WHY THE DOCTRINE?

The objective of the Doctrine of Ultra Virus is to ensure the shareholders and the creditors that the fund and assets of the company will not be used for any purpose other than those specified in the Memorandum. Especially the creditors, while dealing with the company can make themselves aware of the fact whether his transaction with the company is an ultra virus or not. If it is found the ultra virus, he can avoid such transaction and thereby safeguard his interest.

4.3.3 EFFECTS OF AN ULTRA VIRUS ACT

The effects of an ultra vires act can be summed up as follows:

1. An ultra vires act will be wholly void and it will not bind the company; neither the company nor the outsider can enforce the contract.
2. Any member of the company can bring an injunction against the company to prevent it from doing any ultra-virus act.
3. The directors of the company will be personally liable to make good the funds used for the ultra virus acts.
4. Where a company's money has been used ultra virus to acquire some property, the right of the company over such property is held secure.
5. Since Ultra Virus contracts are treated as invalid from the outset, they cannot become Intra Virus because of estoppels or ratification.
6. Ultra Virus borrowing does not create a relationship between debtor and creditor. The only possible remedy in such a case is in *ram* and not in *person*.

4.3.4 CAN AN ULTRA VIRUS ACT BE RATIFIED?

An ultra virus act cannot be ratified even by the whole body of the shareholders and make it binding on the company. In other words, even the shareholders cannot do an ultra virus act. This is the peculiar feature of this doctrine.

The principles of law on this subject were first enunciated by Lord Cairons, L.J., in Ashbury Railway Carriage & Iron Co. Ltd. V. Riche. In that case, a company was formed with the following objects:

a. to make, sell, lend or hire, railway carriages and wagons, and
b. to purchase, lease, work and sell mines, minerals and land and buildings.

The directors contracted to finance the construction of a railway line in Belgium with Mls Riche. The Court held that the contract was ultra virus the company and void so that even the subsequent assent of the whole body of the shareholders could not ratify it.

However, later on, the House of Lords held in other cases that the doctrine of ultra vires should be applied reasonably and unless it is expressly prohibited, a company may do an act, which is important for, or incidental to the attainment of its objectives.

4.3.5 TYPES OF ULTRA VIRES ACTS

There are three types of ultra-virus acts. They are-

i. Ultra virus the Memorandum or the company,
ii. Ultra virus the Articles but intra virus the company, and
iii. Ultra virus the directors but intra virus the company.

4.3.6 ULTRA VIRUS THE MEMORANDUM OR THE COMPANY

If the act done or contract made by the company is beyond the powers given in the objects clause of the Memorandum, it is called an act, which is ultra vires the Memorandum. The act is good to the extent of the authority of the company and bad as to the excess. But, where it cannot be separated from the authority conferred on the company by the Memorandum, the whole of the transaction shall be void. However, there is nothing in law to prevent a company from protecting its property, though it is ultra virus to the company.

4.3.7 ULTRA VIRUS THE ARTICLES BUT INTRA VIRUS THE COMPANY

The acts done or contracts made beyond the powers given by the Articles but are within the powers of the Memorandum are called ultra virus the Articles but intra virus the company. The shareholders can ratify these acts by making an alteration in the Articles to that effect.

Ultra Virus the Directors but Intra Virus the Company

These are acts done or contracts made by the directors, which are ultra virus, the directors, but intra virus the company. These acts can be ratified by the company and can make them binding.

4.3.8 IS IT ULTRA VIRES OR ILLEGAL?

The ultra virus act or transaction is different from an illegal act or transaction, although both are voided. An act of a company, which is beyond its objects clause, is ultra virus and, therefore, void, even if it is illegal. Similarly, an illegal act will be void even if it falls within the objects clause. Unfortunately, the doctrine of the ultra virus has often been used in connection with illegal and forbidden acts. This use should also be prevented.

4.4 ARTICLES OF ASSOCIATION

Definition: The **Articles of Association or AOA** are the legal document that along with the memorandum of association serves as the constitution of the company. It is comprised of rules and regulations that govern the company's internal affairs.

The articles of association are concerned with the internal management of the company and aim at carrying out the objectives mentioned in the memorandum. These define the company's purpose and lay out the guidelines of how the task is to be carried out within the organization. The articles of association cover information related to the board of directors, general meetings, voting rights, board proceedings, etc.

The articles of association are the contracts between the shareholders and the organization and among the shareholder themselves. This document often defines the manner in which the shares are to be issued, dividends to be paid, the financial records to be audited and the power to be given to the shareholders with the voting rights.

The articles of association can be considered as the user manual for the organization that comprises the methodology that can be used to accomplish the company's day-to-day operations. This document is binding on the shareholders and the organization and has nothing to do with outsiders. Thus, the company is not accountable for any claims made by any external party.

4.4.1THE ARTICLES OF ASSOCIATION ARE COMPRISED OF THE FOLLOWING PROVISIONS:

- Share capital, call of share, forfeiture of share, conversion of share into stock, transfer of shares, share warrant, surrender of shares, etc.
- Directors, their qualifications, appointment, remuneration, powers, and proceedings of the board of directors meetings.
- Voting rights of shareholders, by poll or proxies and proceeding of shareholders general meetings.
- Dividends and reserves, accounts and audits, borrowing powers and winding up.

4.4.2 IT IS MANDATORY FOR THE FOLLOWING TYPES OF COMPANIES TO HAVE THEIR OWN ARTICLES:

1. **Unlimited Companies:** The article must state the number of members with which the company is to be registered along with the amount of share capital if any.
2. **Companies Limited by Guarantee:** The article must define the number of members with which the company is to be registered.
3. **Private Companies Limited by Shares:** The private company having the share capital, then the article must contain the provision that, restricts the right to transfer shares, limit the number of members to 50, prohibits the invitation to the public for the further subscription of shares in the form of shares or debentures.

Note: In the case of a public company limited by shares, the articles may be framed by the company itself or in case company does not register articles then it might adopt all of any of the regulations as contained in Table A in the Companies Act.

4.4.3 CONTENT

The contents of articles of association should not contradict the Companies Act and the MoA. If the document contains anything contrary to the Companies Act or the Memorandum of Association, it will be inoperative. The pvt concern that are limited by shares and those limited by guarantee and unlimited companies must have their articles of association. Public companies may not have their articles but may adopt Model articles given in Table A of Schedule I of Companies Act, 1956. If a public company has only some articles of its own, for the rest, articles of Table A will be applicable.

Articles that are profound to be registered should be printed, segmented well and sequenced consecutively. Each subscriber to the Memorandum of Association must sign the articles in the presence of at least one witness.

Contents of Articles of Association

The articles generally deal with the following

1. Classes of shares, their values and the rights attached to each of them.

2. Calls on shares, transfer of shares, forfeiture, conversion of shares and alteration of capital.
3. Directors, their appointment, powers, duties etc.
4. Meetings and minutes, notices etc.
5. Accounts and Audit
6. Appointment of and remuneration to Auditors.
7. Voting, poll, proxy etc.
8. Dividends and Reserves
9. Procedure for winding up.
10. Borrowing powers of Board of Directors and managers etc.
11. Minimum subscription.
12. Rules regarding use and custody of the common seal.
13. Rules and regulations regarding conversion of fully paid shares into stock.
14. Lien on shares.

4.4.4 ALTERATION OF ARTICLES OF ASSOCIATION

The alteration of the Articles should not sanction anything illegal. They should be for the benefit of the company. They should not lead to a breach of contract with third parties. The following are the regulations regarding alteration of articles:

A company may alter its Articles with a special resolution. Due importance and care should be given to ensure that the alteration of AoA does not conflict with the provisions of the Memorandum of Association or the Companies Act. A copy of every special resolution altering the Articles must be filed with the Registrar within 30 days of its passing.

1. The proposed alteration should not contravene the provisions of the Companies Act.
2. The proposed alteration should not contravene the provisions of the Memorandum of Association.
3. The alteration should not propose anything illegal.
4. The alteration should be bonafide for the benefit of the company.
5. The proposed alteration should in no way increase the liability of existing members.
6. Alteration can be made only by a special resolution.
7. Alteration can be done with retrospective effect.
8. The Court does not have any power to order the alteration of the Articles of Association.

4.5 DOCTRINE OF CONSTRUCTIVE NOTICE

The doctrine of Constructive notice protects the company from outsiders. It was introduced to protect the company from outsiders of company. The memorandum of association and articles of association of every company need to register with the Registrar of companies. After registering the documents with the registrar of the company, it becomes public documents. It's because the office of the registrar is a public office.

They are open and accessible to all. So, it's necessary for every person dealing with a company to inspect and understand the memorandum and Articles of Association. Even if a person does not read the public documents of the company, it's assumed he has read the public documents of the company. It's presumed by the company that he knows the contents of those documents.

Further, it adds that the person dealing with the company is not only presumed to know the contents of public documents of the company but also understand them according to their real meaning and intention. For instance, he should not only know the powers of the company but also the powers of the officer behind the company. According to Palmer, the principle applies only to the documents which affect the powers of the company.

The common law doctrine of constructive notice applies to all public documents of the company. It contains all the important details of directors, managers, secretaries etc of the company. It also contains the Audited accounts of the company. The doctrine protects the company from outsiders.

There is no relief if a person claims that he has not read the memorandum and article of the association before dealing with the company. Under this doctrine, the company plays safe. It affects the outsiders who deal with the company and faces some problem after dealing the company.

4.5.1 DOCTRINE OF INDOOR MANAGEMENT

The doctrine of indoor management evolved 150 years ago. It's also known as Turquand's rule. The role of the doctrine of indoor management is opposed to that of the rule of constructive notice. The Doctrine of Constructive Notice protects a company from outsiders. Whereas, the Doctrine of Indoor management protects outsiders from the company.

The outsider has no clue how the internal part of the company works. He presumes that there are no irregularities in the internal machinery of the company. This doctrine is also a possible safeguard against the possibility of abusing the doctrine of constructive notice.

A person contracting with the company only needs to inspect the memorandum and article of association of the company. He is not required to inspect internal irregularities. If there are any internal irregularities then the company's liability is to compensate him for any loss. But a person needs to act in good faith and not know about the internal irregularities of the company. This doctrine protects the outsider from the company as he is unaware of the activities which happen behind the closed door of the company.

4.5.2 ORIGIN OF THE DOCTRINE

This doctrine was laid down in the case of Royal British Bank V. Turquand

The directors of the company borrowed some money from the plaintiff. The article of the company provides for the borrowing of money on bonds but there was a necessary condition that a resolution should be passed in a general meeting. Now in this case shareholders claim that as there was no such resolution passed in the general meeting so the company is not bound to pay the money. It was held that the company is bound to pay back the loan. As directors could borrow but be subjected to the resolution, the plaintiff had the right to infer that the necessary resolution must have been passed.

It was held that Turquand can sue the company on the strength of the bond. As he was entitled to assume that the necessary resolution had been passed. Lord Hatherly observed- "Outsiders are bound to know the external position of the company, but are not bound to know its indoor management."

4.5.3 EXCEPTIONS TO DOCTRINE OF INDOOR MANAGEMENT

Following are the exception to the doctrine of Indoor Management:

1. Knowledge of irregularity

The first exception to this doctrine is that the person dealing with the company should not have any knowledge about the internal irregularities of the company. Knowledge of irregularity arises from the fact that the person contracting was himself a party to the inside procedure. The principle is clear that a person who is himself a part of the internal machinery cannot take advantage of irregularities.

2. Forgery

The doctrine of indoor management does not apply to forgery because forgery is void ab- initio. Lord Loreburn said: "It's quite true that persons dealing with limited liability companies are not bound to inquire into their indoor management. But not affected by irregularities of the company if they do not know such irregularities. It cannot apply to a forgery.

3. Negligence on the part of the outsider

If the loss is suffered due to negligence of an outsider, relief can not be claimed under the doctrine of Indoor Management. If the person dealing with the company already had a hint about the internal irregularities of the company and still neglected the irregularities, he enters into a contract with the company, then he cannot claim under the doctrine of Indoor Management.

CHAPTER FIVE

RAISING OF SHARE CAPITAL

Raising of Share Capital: Prospectus – Definition – Registration - Contents – Shelf Prospectus – Deemed Prospectus – Statement in Lieu of Prospectus - Misstatement and their Consequences – Share Capital – Meaning – Kinds – Alteration of Share Capital.

5.1 RAISING OF SHARE CAPITAL

Share capital is the money a company raises by issuing common or preferred stock. The amount of share capital or equity financing a company has can change over time with additional public offerings.

The term share capital can mean slightly different things depending on the context. Accountants have a much narrower definition and their definition rules on the balance sheets of public companies. It means the total amount raised by the company in sales of shares.

5.1.1 PROCEDURE OF RAISING SHARE CAPITAL

(a) Application for Shares:

As stated earlier, after obtaining Certificate of Incorporation, a private company can commence its business. A private company is prohibited from making any invitation to the public to subscribe for any share, or debentures of the company. However, to collect capital from the public, a public company issues a document called. Prospectus, The prospectus is simply an invitation to an offer but is not an offer. It describes the soundness of the business the company proposes to undertake, and the security and profitability of the capital invested in the venture.

On the basis of information furnished in the prospectus, the prospective investors fill out the application forms and forward them to the company's bankers along with the cheques/drafts for the amounts payable on the application. The money payable with the application form is known as the Application Money and must not be less than 5 percent of the nominal value of shares. Applications are not accepted after the last date fixed for the receipt of applications.

(b) Allotment of Shares:

After the last date for the receipt of applications expires, the Board of Directors takes a decision as to the acceptance or rejection of applications. If the share applications are accepted by the company, then shares are said to have been allotted and thereby, there arises a contract between the company and prospective investor. After the acceptance of the application, the applicant becomes a shareholder of the company. The money to be paid by the shareholder on the allotment of shares is called Allotment Money.

(c) Letter of Allotment and Regret:

A letter of allotment, bearing a stamp, is sent to the shareholders who have been allotted shares. A letter of regret together with the application money is sent to those applicants to whom no shares are allotted.

(d) Calls on Shares:

The balance left after application and allotment money is termed as 'call money. Suppose the share is Rs 10 each. Application money is Rs 2 and allotment money is Rs 4, the balance of Rs 4 (i.e. Rs 10-2-4) is 'call money. The call money may be called in a lump sum or it may be called in instalments. Any number of calls First call, the Second call.

The third call and final call may be made to get the full face value of shares.

The following legal provisions must be kept in mind while making calls:

(i) Call money should not exceed 25% of the face value

(ii) There must be a gap of at least one month in making of two calls.

(iii)The call must be made strictly according to the provisions of the Articles of Association

(iv) There should be at least 14 days' notice specifying the shareholders to pay the number of calls.

The Companies Act, 2013 defines a prospectus under *section 2(70)*. A prospectus can be defined as "any document which is described or issued as a prospectus". This also includes any notice, circular, advertisement or any other document acting as an invitation to offers from the public. Such an invitation to offer should be for the purchase of any securities of a corporate body. Shelf prospectus and red herring prospectus are also considered as a prospectus.

5.2 PROSPECTUS

Meaning of Prospectus

Sec. 2(36) of the Companies Act describes a prospectus as "any document issued as a prospectus and includes any notice, circular, advertisement or other document inviting deposits from the public or inviting offers from the public for the subscription or purchase of any share in, or debentures of a body corporate."

In other words, it is a document which invites deposits from the public or invites offers from the public for the subscription of shares in, or debentures of, a company. The words "inviting deposits from the public" were added by the Companies (Amendment) Act, 1974.

5.2.1 FEATURES AND CHARACTERISTICS OF PROSPECTUS

(i) It is a document issued as a prospectus;

(ii) It is an invitation to the member of the public;

(iii) The public is invited to subscribe to the shares or debentures of the company;

(iv) It includes any notice, circular, or advertisement inviting deposits from the public;

(v) It is a document by which the company procures its share capital needed to carry on its activities.

5.2.2 ESSENTIALS FOR A DOCUMENT TO BE CALLED AS A PROSPECTUS

For any document to be considered as a prospectus, it should satisfy two conditions.

1. The document should invite the subscription to public shares or debentures, or it should invite deposits.
2. Such an invitation should be made to the public.
3. The invitation should be made by the company or on behalf company.
4. The invitation should relate to shares, debentures or such other instruments.

5.2.3 OBJECTIVES OF ISSUING PROSPECTUS

1. To bring to the notice of the public that a new company has been formed.

2. To preserve authentic record of the terms and allotment on which the public has been invited to buy its shares or debentures.

3. To secure that the directors of the company accept responsibility for the statements in the prospectus.

Requirements of a Correct Prospectus

The correct prospectus must have the following

1. It must not be exaggerated
2. It must contain full and honest disclosures
3. Material facts must be disclosed and should not be concealed.
4. There must not be false details and untrue statements.

5.3 FORMS AND CONTENTS OF THE PROSPECTUS

Sec. 56 states that every prospectus must

i. State the matters specified in Part I of Schedule II, and

ii. Set out the reports specified in Part II of Schedule II.

Part I of Schedule II—Matters to be Specified:

(a) The contents of the Memorandum:

It expresses the name of the company, objects, nature of business, share capital and its division, liability of members, names and addresses of the signatories and the number of shares subscribed by them.

(b) The qualification shares of the Directors:

If the Articles of the company provide that a certain minimum number of shares to be possessed by the directors as qualification, in that case, a person shall not be qualified to act as a director unless he holds such a number of shares.

(c) No. of redeemable preference shares:

Particulars regarding debentures and redeemable preference shares with their date of redemption must be stated.

(d) Remuneration of the Directors and Promoters:

The prospectus must contain the rate of remuneration for attending meetings and for other services of the Directors and Promoters.

(e) The names, descriptions and addresses of the Directors and Managing Directors:

The names, addresses, descriptions, occupations of the Directors, Managing Directors, Managers and the provisions regarding their appointment must be stated.

(f) The Minimum Subscription:

The minimum subscription on which the directors may proceed to allotment and the amount payable on application, allotment etc. on each share should also be stated in the prospectus.

(g) Time of opening:

The time of the opening of the subscription list should also be stated.

(h) Names and Addresses:

The names and addresses of vendors, if any, and the mode of payment of purchase price and goodwill should also be contained in the prospectus.

(i) Underwriting Commission, Brokerage etc.:

The names of underwriters and the opinion of the directors regarding their financial position and business integrity should also be stated clearly.

(j) Names of the auditors with their addresses:

The reputation of the auditors is also an important factor necessary for public patronage.

(k) Particular of Contracts:

The dates of and parties to every material contract, and reasonable time and place of its inspection are also significant.

(l) Preliminary Expenses:

The estimated amount of preliminary expenses to be incurred should also be furnished.

(m) Particulars of Directors:

Full particulars of the nature and interest of every director or promoter in the promotion of or in the property proposed to be acquired by the company within two years with a statement of all sums paid or agreed to be paid to him in cash or shares for service rendered.

(n) Disclosure:

Full disclosure on these matters should also be made in the prospectus.

(o) Expected rate of dividend and voting rights:

The rights of shareholders relating to voting, meeting and dividends along with the nature and extent of restrictions to be imposed by the Articles on their right to transfer shares should also be stated in clear and convincing terms.

(p) Capitalization of Profits and Surplus from revaluation of assets:

Capitalization of profits/reserves of a company or if any of its subsidiaries have been capitalized (i.e. issuing bonus shares)— particular of such capitalization and also surplus, if any, assets from the revaluation of assets should also be stated.

(q) Inspection of Balance Sheet and Profit and Loss Account:

The following reports are to be annexed:

Part II of Schedule II— Reports to be set out:

(a) Report by the Auditor:

An audit report of the company relating to:

(i) Its profits .and losses, assets and liabilities,

(ii) The dividend paid by the company during the five financial years preceding the issue of the prospectus should also be furnished.

(b) Report by the Accountant:

The accountant should also state a report relating to profits or losses and assets and liabilities on a date which must not be more than 120 days before the date of issue of the prospectus.

5.6 STATEMENT IN LIEU OF PROSPECTUS

Every public company either issue a prospectus or file a statement in lieu of a prospectus. This is not mandatory for a private company. But when a private company converts from a private to a public company, it must have either filed a prospectus if earlier issued or it has to file a statement in lieu of a prospectus.

The provisions regarding the statement in lieu of prospectus have been stated under *section 70* of the Companies Act 2013.

If a public company does not invite the public to subscribe to its shares but acquires to have money from private sources it may not issue a prospectus. In the circumstances, the promoters are required to prepare a draft prospectus which is known as a 'Statement in lieu of Prospectus' which must contain the information required to be disclosed by Schedule III of the Act.

Sec. 70(1) states that a company having a share capital which does not issue a prospectus shall not allot any of its shares or debentures unless at least 3 days before the allotment of shares or debentures there has been delivered to the Registrar for registration a statement in lieu of prospectus.

The statement shall be signed by every person who is named therein as a director or proposed director of the company or by his authorised agent in writing. It shall be in the form and contain particulars set out in Schedule III of the Act.

Sec. 70(4) lays down that, in contravention of Sec. 70(1), the company and every director of the company, who wilfully authorizes or permits the contravention shall be punishable with a fine which may extend to Rs. 1,000.

Similarly, Sec. 70(5) also states that where the statement in lieu of prospectus contains any untrue statement, the persons responsible, for the issue thereof, may be punished by imprisonment which may extend to 2 years or with a fine which may extend to Rs. 5,000, or with both.

Advertisement of Prospectus:

Section 30 of the Companies Act 2013 contains the provisions regarding the advertisement of the prospectus. This section states that when in any manner the advertisement of a prospectus is published, it is mandatory to specify the contents of the memorandum of the company regarding the object, member's liabilities, amount of the company's share capital, signatories and the number of shares subscribed by them and the capital structure of the company. Types of prospectus are as follows.

- Red Herring Prospectus
- Shelf Prospectus
- Abridged prospectus
- Deemed Prospectus

Shelf Prospectus:

A shelf prospectus can be defined as a prospectus that has been issued by any public financial institution, company or bank for one or more issues of securities or class of securities as mentioned in the prospectus. When a shelf prospectus is issued then the issuer does not need to issue a separate prospectus for each offering he can offer or sell securities without issuing any further prospectus.

The provisions related to shelf prospectus have been discussed under *section 31* ***of the Companies Act, 2013.***

The regulations are to be provided by the Securities and Exchange Board of India for any class or classes of companies that may file a shelf prospectus at the stage of the first offer of securities to the registrar.

The prospectus shall prescribe the validity period of the prospectus and it should be not be exceeding one year. This period commences from the opening date of the first offer of the securities. For any second or further offer, no separate prospectus is required.

While filing for a shelf prospectus, a company is required to file an information memorandum along with it.

Red Herring Prospectus:

Red herring prospectus is the prospectus which lacks complete particulars about the quantum of the price of the securities. A company may issue a red herring prospectus **prior to the issue of a prospectus** when it is proposing to make an offer of securities.

This type of prospectus needs to be filed with the registrar at least three days prior to the opening of the subscription list or the offer. The obligations carried by a red herring prospectus are the same as a prospectus. If there is any variation between a red herring prospectus and a prospectus then it should be highlighted in the prospectus as variations.

When the offer of securities closes then the prospectus has to state the total capital raised either raised by the way of debt or share capital. It also has to state the closing price of the securities. Any other details which have not been included in the prospectus need to be registered with the registrar and SEBI.

The applicant or subscriber has the right under *Section60B(7)* to withdraw the application on any intimation of variation within 7 days of such intimation and the withdrawal should be communicated in writing.

Abridged Prospectus:

The abridged prospectus is a summary of a prospectus filed before the registrar. It contains all the features of a prospectus. An abridged prospectus contains all the information of the prospectus in brief so that it should be convenient and quick for an investor to know all the useful information in short.

Section33(1) of the Companies Act, 2013 also states that when any form for the purchase of securities of a company is issued, it must be accompanied by an abridged prospectus.

It contains all the useful and materialistic information so that the investor can take a rational decision and it also reduces the cost of public issue of the capital as it is a short form of a prospectus.

Deemed Prospectus:

A deemed prospectus has been stated under *section 25(1) of the Companies Act, 2013.*

When any company offers securities for sale to the public, allots or agrees to allot securities, the document will be considered as a deemed prospectus through which the offer is made to the public for sale. The document is deemed to be a prospectus of a company for all purposes and all the provision of content and liabilities of a prospectus will be applied to it.

In the case of *SEBI v. Kunnamkulam Paper Mills Ltd.*, it was held by the court that where a rights issue is made to the existing members with a right to renounce in the favour of others, it becomes a deemed prospectus if the number of such others exceeds fifty.

Registration of prospectus:

Section26(7) states the registration of a prospectus by the registrar. **According to this section, when the registrar can register a prospectus when:**

1. It fulfils the requirements of this section, i.e., section 26 of the Companies Act, 2013; and
2. It contains the consent of all the persons named in the prospectus in writing.

Issue of prospectus after registration

If a prospectus is not issued within 90 days from the date from which a copy was delivered before the registrar, then it is considered to be invalid.

Contravention of section

If a prospectus is issued in contravention of the provision under section 26 of the Companies Act 2013, then the company can be punished under *section 26(9)*. The punishment for the contravention is:

- Fine of not less than Rs. 50,000 extending up to 3,00,000.

If any person becomes aware of such prospectus after knowing the fact that such prospectus is being issued in contravention of section 26 then he is punishable with the following penal provisions.

- Imprisonment up to a term of 3 years, or
- Fine of more than Rs. 50,000 not exceeding Rs. 3,00,000.

5.7 MIS-STATEMENTS IN PROSPECTUS

Mis-statements and false statements in the prospectus are instruments by which dishonest company promoters may practice fraud on the public money. In order to prevent this practice the law imposes certain duties and liabilities on those persons who are responsible for such issues.

If, however, the prospectus contains any misstatement of a material fact or if the prospectus wants in any material fact, two types of liabilities will arise.

They are:

(1) Civil Liability

(2) Criminal Liability

Before discussing the above we are to know the liability which may arise for an Untrue Statement. It is the duty of the authors of the prospectus to see that the prospectus does not contain any untrue statements which may mislead the public.

According to Sec. 65 of the Companies Act, Untrue Statement' in connection with a prospectus shall deem to include:

(i) A statement which is misleading in the form and context in which it is included, and

(ii) An omission which is calculated to mislead.

In short, an untrue statement means and includes any statement which is not only a false statement but also a statement which creates a wrong impression of actual fact. Concealment of material fact is also treated as mis-statement or untrue statement.

Now we are going to highlight the civil and criminal liabilities that may appear due to misstatement in the prospectus:

(1) Civil Liability:

Sec. 62(1) of the Companies Act states that such persons are liable to pay compensation for any loss or damage which any person may suffer from the purchase of any share or debenture on the basis of the untrue statement. Consequently, a person who has suffered a loss may claim a contribution from the others who were associated relating to the issue of a prospect until it appears that he was guilty of fraud while the others were not proved to be guilty.

(2) Criminal Liability:

According to Sec. 63(1) of the Companies Act, every person who has authorised the issue of a prospectus containing untrue statements shall be punishable with imprisonment which may extend to two years or with a fine which may extend to Rs. 5,000—or both.

(3) Penalty:

Sec. 68 of the Companies Act provides that a person shall not, either knowingly or recklessly, by making any statement, promise or forecast which is false, deceptive or misleading or, by any dishonest concealment of material facts, induce or attempt to induce another person to enter into or to offer to enter into any

(i) agreement for acquiring, disposing-off, subscribing for or underwriting shares or debentures;

(ii) agreement, the purpose or pretended purpose of which is to secure a profit to any of the parties from the yield of shares or debentures, or by inference to fluctuations in the value of shares or debentures.

Otherwise, he shall be punishable with imprisonment for a term which may extend to 5 years or with a fine which may extend to Rs. 10,000—or with both.

Persons who are liable for untrue statements in the prospectus:

According to Sec. 62 (1) of the Companies Act, the following persons are liable and punishable for untrue statements in the prospectus:

(a) Every person who is a director of the company at the time of the issue of the prospectus;

(b) Every person who has authorized himself to be named and is named in the prospectus either as a director or as having agreed to become a director, either immediately or after some time;

(c) Every person who is a promoter of the company; and

(d) Every person who has authorized the issues of the prospectus.

Defence available in an action on the prospectus:

The parties against whom the proceeding has been taken for misstatement in the prospectus may use certain pleas as their defence:

1. DE fences against Civil Liability:

According to Sec. 62(2) of the Companies Act, no decree for damage shall be passed if the person charged can prove any one of the followings:

(a) Withdrawal of consent:

A person is not liable if he withdrew his consent before the issue of the prospectus.

(b) Issue without knowledge and consent:

If the person can prove that the prospectus was issued without his knowledge or consent and, after becoming aware of its issues, he gave public notice that the same was issued without his knowledge and consent.

(c) Statement of an expert:

If the statement which is alleged to be untrue purports to be a statement of an expert or a copy or a valuation report of an expert, the person charged can be discharged from his liability if he can prove:

(i) It is a fair and correct copy or representation or extract of the expert's statement;

(ii) He had reasonable grounds to believe;

(iii) The expert had given his consent to the issue of the prospectus;

(iv) The expert had not withdrawn his consent before registration.

(d) True Statement:

The person charged can escape from his liability if he can prove that he had reasonable ground to believe and did, up to the time of the allotment of shares or debentures, believe that the statement was true.

2. Defences available to an expert:

Sec. 62(4) states that an expert whose opinion was included in the prospectus can use the following as defence:

(a) Withdrawal of consent:

After giving consent, he withdrew it in writing before delivery of a copy of the prospectus for registration.

(b) Knowledge of untrue statement:

If the person, on becoming aware of the untrue statement, withdrew his consent in writing and gave public notice with reasons thereof, after delivery of the copy of the prospectus to and before allotment.

(c) True statement:

He was competent to make such statement and he had reasonable grounds to believe and did up to the time of the allotment of shares and debentures, believe that the statement was true.

3. Defense's against Criminal Liability:

Sec. 63(1) states that a person charged in a criminal court will be acquitted if he can prove any one of the following:

(a) That the statement was immaterial, or

(b) That he had reasonable grounds to believe and did, up to the time of the issue of the prospectus, believe that the statement was true.

5.7.1 PROCESS FOR FILING AND ISSUING A PROSPECTUS

Application Forms:

As stated under **section 33,** the application form for the securities is issued only when they are accompanied by a memorandum with all the features of the prospectus referred to as an abridged prospectus.

The exceptions to this rule are:

- When an application form is issued as an invitation to a person to enter into an underwriting agreement regarding securities.
- Application issued for the securities not offered to the public.

Contents:

For filing and issuing the prospectus of a public company, it must be signed and dated and contain all the necessary information as stated under *section 26 of the Companies Act,2013*:

1. Name and registered address of the office, its secretary, auditor, legal advisor, bankers, trustees, etc.
2. Date of the opening and closing of the issue.
3. Statements of the Board of Directors about separate bank accounts where receipts of issues are to be kept.
4. Statement of the Board of Directors about the details of utilization and non-utilisation of receipts of previous issues.
5. Consent of the directors, auditors, and bankers to the issue, and expert opinions.
6. Authority for the issue and details of the resolution passed for it.
7. Procedure and time scheduled for the allotment and issue of securities.
8. The capital structure of the in the manner which may be prescribed.
9. The objective of a public offer.

10. The objective of the business and its location.
11. Particulars related to risk factors of the specific project, gestation period of the project, any pending legal action and other important details related to the project.
12. Minimum subscription and what amount is payable on the premium.
13. Details of directors, their remuneration and the extent of their interest in the company.
14. Reports for financial information such as auditor's report, report of profit and loss of the five financial years, business and transaction reports, statement of compliance with the provisions of the Act and any other report.

Filing of Copy with the Registrar:

As stated under ***sub-section 4 of** section26 **of the Companies Act, 2013***, the prospectus is not to be issued by a company or on its behalf unless on or before the date of publication, a copy of the prospectus is delivered to the registrar for registration.

The copy should be signed by every person whose name has been mentioned in the prospectus as a director or proposed director or the assigned attorney on his behalf.

Delivery of Copy of the Prospectus to the Registrar:

As per *section26(6) **of the Companies Act 2013***, the prospectus should mention that its copy has been delivered to the registrar on its face. The statement should also mention the document submitted to the registrar along with a copy of the prospectus.

5.8 SHARE CAPITAL

Meaning of Share Capital

The term capital usually means a particular amount of money with which a business is started. In the Indian Companies Act, it has been used in different senses in various parts of the Act, but in general, it means the money subscribed under Memorandum of Association of the Company. Capital represents the assets with which the undertaking is carried on.

The total of the nominal value of shares of a company is known as its share capital. In the case of companies, the terms 'capital' and 'share capital' have been held to be synonymous. Capital is to be stated in the Memorandum of Association and Articles of Association of the Company.

5.8.1 TYPES/NATURE OF SHARE CAPITAL

The share capital of the company may be of the following types:

1. Registered, Authorised or Nominal Capital:

The Memorandum of Association of every company has to specify the amount of capital with which it wants to be registered. The capital so stated is called Registered, Authorized or Nominal Capital. The Registered Capital is the maximum amount of share capital which a company can raise by way of public subscription.

2. Issued Capital:

The company may not issue the entire authorised capital at once. It goes on raising the capital as and when the need for additional funds is felt. So, the issued capital is that part of Authorised/Registered or Nominal Capital which is offered to the public for subscription in the form of shares.

3. Unissued Capital:

The balance of nominal capital remaining to be issued is called Unissued Capital.

4. Subscribed Capital:

It is that part of "issued capital" for which applications are received from the public. The subscribed capital is allotted to the respective subscribers as per the resolution passed by the directors of the company.

5. Called up Capital:

It is that part of subscribed capital which has been called up by the company. A company does not call at once the full amount on each of the shares it has allotted and therefore, calls up only such amount as it needs.

6. Uncalled up Capital:

It is the uncalled portion of the allotted capital and represents the contingent liability of the shareholders on the shares.

7. Paid up Capital:

It is that part of called-up capital against which payment has been received from the members on their respective shares in response to the calls made by the company.

8. Reserve Capital or Reserve Liability:

By Reserve Capital, we mean that amount which is not callable by the company except in the event of the company being wound up. The company cannot demand the payment of money on the shares to that extent during its lifetime. Reserve capital may be created using a special resolution passed by the company in its General Meeting by a three-fourths majority of those voting on it.

When once the Reserve Capital has been so created the company cannot alter its Articles of Association to make the reserve liability available at any time. The Reserve Capital cannot be charged as security for loans by the directors. It cannot be turned into ordinary capital without the order of the court. It cannot be cancelled at the time of reduction of capital.

9. Fixed Capital:

The fixed capital of a company is what the company retains in the shape of fixed assets such as land and buildings, plant and machinery, furniture, etc.

10. Circulating Capital:

The circulating capital is a part of subscribed capital which is circulated in business in the form of using goods or other assets such as book debts, bill receivables, cash, bank balance, etc.

Classes of Share Capital:

The share capital of a company limited by shares may be of the following two kinds:

1. Preference share capital, and
2. Equity share capital.

1. Preference Share Capital:

It means that part of the capital of the company which:

(a) Carries a preferential right as to payment of dividends at a fixed rate during the lifetime of the company.

(b) Carries, on the winding up of the company, a preferential right to be repaid the amount of the capital paid up.

2. Equity Share Capital:

It means concerning a company, limited by shares, all share capital which is not preference share capital.

5.8.3 ALTERATION OF SHARE CAPITAL UNDER COMPANIES ACT, 2013

The capital of a company is separated into units of a fixed denomination and such unit is a share. A share in the share capital of a company includes stock which is defined under Section 2(84).

Section 2(8) of The Companies Act 2013, defines that "Authorised capital" or "nominal capital" means such capital which is authorized by the memorandum of a company to be the maximum amount of share capital of the company. The companies are allowed to alter the authorized share capital according to the procedures mentioned in Sections 61 to 64 read with Sections 13 and 14 of the Companies Act. An increase or decrease in the share capital of a company may be carried out as and when the company requires thus leading to an alteration in the company's share capital. The alterations to the capital clause have to be done according to the Companies Act, 2013.

The procedure involved in altering the Share Capital

1. It has to be confirmed whether a company is authorized to increase its share capital according to the Articles of Association (AOA) and if it does not authorize then the procedure for such alteration has o be carried out.
2. A board meeting should be called for an Extraordinary General Meeting (EGM) to get the approval of the shareholders for such an alteration.
3. The EGM should be called comprising of the shareholders by sending a notice mentioning the purpose of the scheduled meeting regarding the alteration of the MOA and AOA thus altering the Share capital of the company.
4. The Special resolution shall be passed to alter the MOA and AOA thus altering the Share Capital of the Company.
5. Authorising the board to file necessary forms and resolutions with the Registrar of Companies (ROC) having jurisdiction.
6. The e- form SH-7 with ROC on payment of a stipulated fee.

Once the AOA has been altered the board meeting has to be called by the company. Every member, legal representative or the assignee, the auditor(s) and every director of the company has to be given a notice 21 days before the actual date of the meeting. The notice shall be written or in an electric form. The general meeting can also be convened at a shorter notice if 95 percent of the members who are allowed to vote at the meeting give their consent in the manner prescribed written or electronic.

The place of the meeting, the date of the meeting and the hour of the meeting shall be specified in the notice along with the business agenda of the meeting which is mentioned under Section 101 of the Companies Act. Along with the notice, a statement should be attached therewith specifying the particulars and objects regarding every point of extraordinary business to be carried on at the general meeting, concerning the financial or any other kind of interest related to all the directors and the managers and people related to the key managerial persons according to section 102 of the CA, 2013.

Once the formalities of the notice have been complied with the company shall call an EGM and the members have to vote either in favour or against the alteration of the authorized share capital. An ordinary resolution is passed by the board members after holding the EGM.

Alteration of the MOA and AOA:

1. The power of a limited company to alter its share capital is given under Section 61 of the Companies Act, 2013. Sub-clause further states that a limited company having a share capital may, if so authorized by its articles, alter its memorandum in its general meeting to Increase its authorized share capital by such amount as it thinks expedient
2. The authorized share capital of the company can be increased by altering the memorandum of association. The provisions regarding the alteration of the memorandum of association and Articles of association are given under Section 13 and 14 of the Companies Act respectively.
3. A company may alter the provisions of the memorandum after it has passed a special resolution thus complying with the procedural requirements given under Section 13.
4. An alteration has to be made in the Memorandum Of Association and the Articles Of Association under clause 5 and 4 respectively.
5. According to Clause 5 ‘, The Authorized Share Capital of the company is INR 1,00,000/- divided into 10,000 Equity Shares of INR 10 each. The minimum paid up share capital of the company is INR 1,00,000.
6. Alteration of AOA with regards to increasing share capital is given under Clause 4.
7. Section 14 of the Companies Act, 2013 also states that where the company does not have the authority to amend its AOA then the alteration can be carried out by the procedure of passing a special resolution.
8. Section 14 states that the alteration to a company's articles can be done only by passing a special resolution and the order of approval of the alteration carried out has to be filed with the ROC accompanied by the hard copy of the altered articles not later than fifteen days in the manner which is prescribed. The alteration is only valid if there was a provision in the original articles

Registrar to be given Notice:

The registrar of companies shall be notified within thirty days from such alteration and a copy of the altered memorandum has to be provided as well. In case of default by the company or any of its officers, the company or its officers shall be liable and punishable with a fine which may extend up to a thousand rupees for each day of delay or rupees five lakh whichever is less. The above provision is given under Section 64 of the Companies Act.

Purpose of the form

Whenever a company alters its share capital or number of members independently or increases the share capital by conversion of debentures/loans due to the order of the Central Government, then a return shall be filed with the registrar within 30 days of such alteration. The return shall also be filed where the company redeems any redeemable preference shares.

Stamp duty can be paid electronically through the MCA portal and the following documents are to be attached

1. Notice of extraordinary general meeting
2. Certified true copy of the ordinary resolution
3. Altered Memorandum of association
4. Altered AOA, if any.

E-Form MGT 14 to be filed:

While the filing of Form MGT- 14 the provisions mentioned under section 117 (1) and Section 192 of The Companies Act 2013 have to be dealt with. Under sub-section 3 clause 1 of Section 117, the provision mentioned therein also applies to a special resolution.

A copy of all the decisions taken concerning the matters which are specified under subsection 3 along with the explanations under section 102 shall be attached therewith to the notice convening the EGM in which the proposed resolution shall be passed and should be filed with the registrar not exceeding thirty days along with the stipulated fees which have to be paid as specified under Section 403 of the Companies Act.

Section 117(1) states that a copy of the resolution which has the effect of altering the articles and a copy of every agreement referred to in sub-section 3 shall be attached to every copy of the articles issued after passing of the resolution or making of the agreement.

Repercussions of not Filing the Form:

According to section 117 (2) where the company fails to comply with the provisions mentioned in sub-section (1) the company shall be liable to pay a fine which shall not be less than five lakh rupees and may extend up to twenty-five lakh rupees. Each officer of the company who has defaulted along with the liquidator of the company shall be liable to pay a fine of rupees one lakh which may extend up to five lakh rupees.

Printed by Libri Plureos GmbH in Hamburg,
Germany